A LEG AT EACH CORNER

FOR
PENELOPE

New York, E. P. Dutton & Co., Inc., 1971

PRINTED IN GREAT BRITAIN
© NORMAN THELWELL 1962

This drawing reproduced by permission of the Proprietors of *Punch*

CONTENTS

HOW TO GET A PONY	*page* 7
LEARNING TO RIDE	17
GROOMING	33
SCHOOLING	45
HEALTH	59
BREEDS	73
SHOW JUMPING	81
HUNTING	101
POINTS TO REMEMBER	113

How To Get A Pony

ACQUIRING A PONY IS NOT QUITE SO EASY AS IT SOUNDS..

IT IS AGAINST THE LAW TO TAKE THEM FROM THE NEW FOREST

— AND RISKY TO BUY THEM FROM PUBLIC AUCTIONS.

SO LOOK OUT FOR ONE WHICH A FRIEND HAS GROWN OUT OF —

OR BUY ONE FROM SOMEONE YOU TRUST

WHEN CHOOSING...

GOOD FEET ARE MOST IMPORTANT

— AND GOOD MANNERS ESSENTIAL

— THE EYES WILL TELL YOU MORE THAN ANY OTHER FEATURE...

BUT EXPERT ADVICE IS NEEDED AS DEFECTS ARE OFTEN COVERED UP.

SOME PONIES DO NOT MOVE WELL —

SOME DO NOT MOVE AT ALL

YOU WILL LEARN A GREAT DEAL FROM A GLANCE

AT HIS TEETH AND REMEMBER —

NEVER BUY A HORSE THAT WHISTLES.

YOU WONT FIND YOUR PERFECT
PONY STRAIGHT AWAY —
BUT SOONER OR LATER...

... HE'LL FIND YOU.

LEARNING TO RIDE

POINTS OF A RIDER

A CHILD IS READY TO RIDE AS SOON AS HE
                                    SHOWS HIMSELF KEEN...

BUT IT IS INADVISABLE
    TO INFLUENCE HIM AGAINST HIS WILL.

THE METHOD OF MOUNTING IS NOT IMPORTANT...

.... SO LONG AS IT IS SAFE.

THE CORRECT SITTING POSITION MUST BE MASTERED

AND EXERCISES CARRIED OUT IN THE SADDLE —

THE NATURAL AIDS TO HORSEMANSHIP ARE THE HANDS, THE LEGS, THE BODY & THE VOICE —

THE ARTIFICIAL AIDS...

ARE WHIPS, SPURS, MARTINGALES
& GAGS

GRIP WILL IMPROVE WITH EXPERIENCE

AND BALANCE WITH PRACTICE —

TALK TO YOUR PONY — HE WILL KNOW WHAT YOU MEAN —

AND SPEND AS MUCH TIME IN HIS COMPANY AS YOU POSSIBLY CAN.

IN SPITE OF OUR
CONSTANT CRITICISM
OF CHILDREN TODAY

THERE IS NO DOUBT
THAT THEY HAVE...

... AS MUCH SPIRIT OF ADVENTURE — DETERMINATION ...

.... AND DOWNRIGHT COURAGE .....

... AS THEIR PARENTS ....

... EVER HAD

GROOMING

MAKE SURE YOUR PONY IS SECURELY TIED

YOU WILL KNOW WHEN HIS COAT NEEDS ATTENTION —

— BUT DON'T CLIP HIM YOURSELF UNLESS
YOU ARE AN EXPERT

BEGIN GROOMING BY REMOVING ALL SURPLUS MUD —

— AND TONE UP HIS MUSCLES BY BANGING
                    WITH A SACK OF WET STRAW

USE THE BODY BRUSH VIGOROUSLY —
        HE WILL ENJOY IT

POLISH HIS COAT WITH A RUBBER

GET HIS TAIL WELL INTO THE BUCKET WHEN SHAMPOOING —

BUT BEWARE OF WASHING THE MANE
JUST BEFORE A SHOW

DETERGENTS SHOULD BE AVOIDED

AND TAIL PULLING UNDERTAKEN WITH CARE

FINISH OFF BY APPLYING BANDAGES TO THE LEGS.

SCHOOLING

A HAPPY PONY THINKS OF YOU AS HIS BEST FRIEND

SO NEVER LOSE YOUR TEMPER OVER SOME
        LITTLE MISTAKE

BUT HAVE SOME TIT·BIT HANDY FOR WHEN
                                                   HE DOES WELL

HE MUST BE TAUGHT TO STAND CORRECTLY —

— TO BE LED WITHOUT FUSS

AND TO MOVE OFF PROMPTLY, WHEN ORDERED TO DO SO

HE WILL QUICKLY GET USED TO HAVING
                    HIS BRIDLE PUT ON —

BUT YOU SHOULD PUT SMALLER WEIGHTS ON HIS BACK BEFORE ATTEMPTING TO MOUNT HIM YOURSELF

MASTERY IS ACHIEVED BY SUBTLETY . . . .

. . . NOT BY ABUSE

BUT AT LEAST TWO PEOPLE MAY BE NECESSARY TO WORK HIM ON THE LUNGE REIN

PONIES ARE NATURAL JUMPERS

BUT DON'T EXPECT MIRACLES TOO EARLY

ENDLESS PATIENCE IS REQUIRED —

AND ABSOLUTE AUTHORITY MUST BE MAINTAINED

ONCE YOU HAVE GAINED YOUR PONY'S RESPECT -
HALF THE BATTLE IS WON

HEALTH

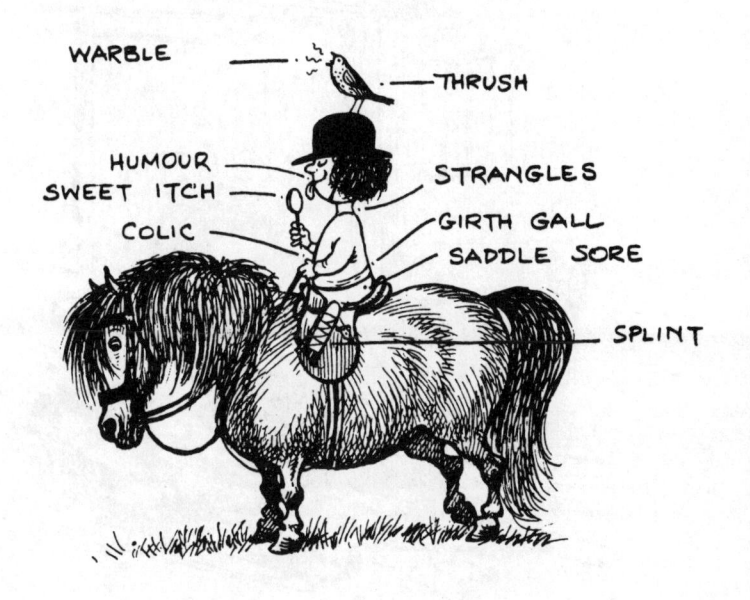

- WARBLE
- THRUSH
- HUMOUR
- SWEET ITCH
- COLIC
- STRANGLES
- GIRTH GALL
- SADDLE SORE
- SPLINT

A FEW COMMON AILMENTS

IF BORED, PONIES DEVELOP TROUBLESOME VICES ...

... SO TRY TO KEEP HIM ENTERTAINED

IF SIMPLE AILMENTS ARE DETECTED —

DON'T PANIC

MAKE HIM WARM AND COMFORTABLE

KEEP A FEW SIMPLE REMEDIES HANDY

AND LEARN HOW TO ADMINISTER THEM

COLDS CAN BE RELIEVED BY INHALING EUCALYPTUS —

AND COUGHS BY SMEARING THE BACK OF THE
TONGUE WITH PASTE

IF HE IS CONSTANTLY TRYING TO SCRATCH HIMSELF,
SUSPECT SKIN TROUBLE

AND IF HE ROLLS ABOUT, IT IS PROBABLY COLIC

SYMPATHETIC NURSING CAN WORK WONDERS –

... BUT DON'T TRY TO REPLACE THE VET

YOU WILL KNOW IT HAS ALL BEEN WORTH IT WHEN HE'S UP AND ABOUT AGAIN.

BREEDS

THE NEW FOREST PONY LIVES ALMOST EXCLUSIVELY ON
A DIET OF LETTUCE, CUCUMBER & FISH-PASTE SANDWICHES

OWING TO THE HARSHNESS OF ITS ENVIRONMENT
THE DARTMOOR HAS BECOME TOUGH & HARDY

THE EXMOOR IS MEALYMOUTHED

THE WELSH MOUNTAIN · OUR MOST BEAUTIFUL
NATIVE BREED · IS INCLINED TO BE A TRIFLE
WIDE IN THE BARREL

THE ANCIENT CONNEMARA WAS HANGING ABOUT GALWAY BAY LONG BEFORE THE SONG WRITERS GOT THERE

FELL & DALE CAN CARRY PRODIGIOUS WEIGHTS WITH EASE

THE HIGHLAND IS USED BY SPORTSMEN TO CARRY THEIR 'BAG' DOWN THE MOUNTAINS

THE SHETLAND - WHICH IS THE WORLDS SMALLEST BREED ...

... IS RESPECTED BY ALL WHO KNOW HORSEFLESH

THERE ARE OTHER PONIES TOO – KNOWN AS
BLOOD PONIES

THEY CAN BE SEEN IN ACTION AT HORSE SHOWS
ALL OVER THE COUNTRY

SHOW JUMPING

COMPETITORS MUST ENTER THE ARENA MOUNTED

THEY MAY ADOPT THE FORWARD SEAT....

.... OR THE BACKWARD SEAT

BUT THEY MUST NOT START UNTIL THE SIGNAL IS GIVEN..

.... OR STOP BEFORE COMPLETING THE COURSE

NO MORE THAN THREE REFUSALS ARE PERMITTED —

AND NO FOOT MUST TOUCH THE WATER

BLINKERS ARE NOT ALLOWED —

AND UNAUTHORISED ASSISTANCE IS PROHIBITED

DON'T EXPECT TO WIN EVERY TIME ......

..... YOUR TURN WILL COME.

*   *   *   *   *

HOW TO TIME YOUR JUMPS

TAKE - OFF
TOO EARLY
◀

TAKE - OFF
TOO LATE
◀

TAKE-OFF JUST RIGHT

THERE IS NO DOUBT AT ALL IN THE
MINDS OF HORSE LOVERS.....

THAT THE LONG HOURS OF PATIENT TRAINING.....

....LABORIOUS WORK....

..... AND CAREFUL GROOMING ....

.... ARE AMPLY REPAID.....

..... BY THE THRILL OF ATTENDING ......

.... A GYMKHANA

HUNTING

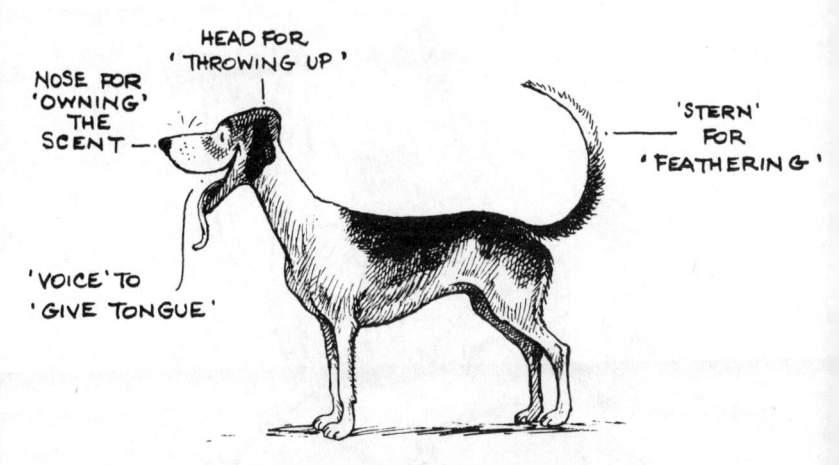

NOSE FOR 'OWNING' THE SCENT

HEAD FOR 'THROWING UP'

'STERN' FOR 'FEATHERING'

'VOICE' TO 'GIVE TONGUE'

A HALF COUPLE OF HOUNDS

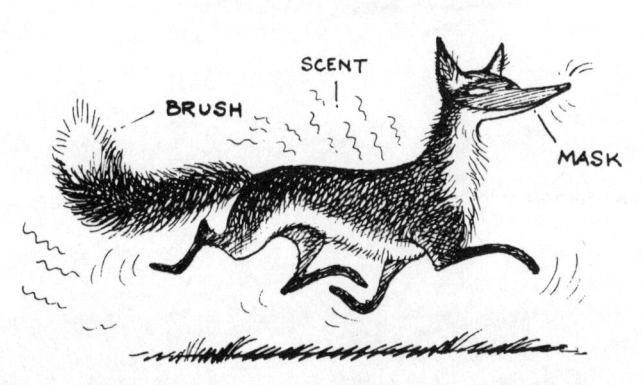

BRUSH

SCENT

MASK

'CHARLES JAMES' OR 'THE VARMINT'

A SMART TURNOUT IS OF FIRST IMPORTANCE.

SEE THAT YOUR PONY ARRIVES AT THE MEET QUITE FRESH

DON'T WAIT UNTIL THE SECRETARY
ASKS BEFORE YOU PAY YOUR 'CAP' —

AND GIVE THE MASTER A POLITE GREETING WHEN YOU SEE HIM

THE FOX IS FREQUENTLY REFERRED TO BY OTHER NAMES —

BUT A HOUND IS A HOUND AND MUST NEVER BE CALLED
                                    ANYTHING ELSE

ALWAYS DO EXACTLY WHAT THE HUNTSMAN TELLS YOU....

AND IF YOU MUST TALK IN THE FIELD —
　　　　　　　　　MAKE IT A WHISPER

DON'T MONOPOLISE THE BEST FENCES —

AND EVEN IF YOU'RE ABLE TO KEEP UP WITH HOUNDS...

YOU'RE NOT A REAL HUNTER UNTIL YOU'VE BEEN BLOODED

Points to Remember

AN UNTIDY RIDER IS AN INSULT TO A HORSE

DO NOTHING WHICH MAY CAUSE HIM ALARM —

BUT HE SHOULD BE INTRODUCED TO THE HAZARDS OF MODERN TRAFFIC

AN ACTIVE PONY WILL NEED SHOEING REGULARLY.

KEEP SOMETHING HANDY TO PICK OUT HIS HOOVES.

MAKE SURE THAT HIS TACK FITS SNUGLY — OR IT MAY CHAFE

AND ALWAYS CHECK THE GIRTH BEFORE YOU MOVE OFF

DON'T JUMP FENCES TOO CLOSE TO TREES —

— OR LEAVE GATES OPEN AFTER GOING THROUGH THEM

KEEP A SHARP LOOKOUT FOR SIGNS OF LICE —

AND IF HE'S A KICKER YOU MUST TIE A RED RIBBON ON HIS TAIL

WHEN YOU WIN SOMETHING -
    DON'T TAKE ALL THE CREDIT YOURSELF...

.... REMEMBER WHO DID MOST OF THE WORK

DON'T KEEP HIM OUT WHEN HE WANTS TO GO HOME

AND ALWAYS ATTEND TO HIS COMFORT BEFORE YOUR OWN

IN SHORT — TREAT YOUR PONY AS YOU LIKE
   TO BE TREATED YOURSELF.

thelwell country

thelwell country

New York, E. P. Dutton & Co., Inc., 1971

PRINTED IN GREAT BRITAIN

© NORMAN THELWELL 1959

for
THOSE WHO ENJOY THE COUNTRY LIFE

Most of the drawings in this book originally appeared in *Punch*; some in the *News Chronicle*. The artist is indebted to the Proprietors of *Punch* and to the Editor of the *News Chronicle* for permission to publish them here.

contents

FOREWORD by H. F. Ellis	*page* 9
THELWELL COUNTRY	11
ITS HORSES	43
ITS BIRD LIFE	63
ITS NOMADS	75
ITS TRADE	85
AND, OF COURSE, ITS PEOPLE	96

"That's *one* Christmas present she won't break in a hurry."

foreword

HUMOROUS artists used to represent the countryside—a few unfortunately still do—as a weird backward region inhabited by unbelievably yokelly yokels and visited by townspeople who were frightened of cows and made fools of themselves with unfamiliar objects like guns and horses. Norman Thelwell never patronises. He knows the country, and assumes that you and I know it too. Thelwell country is real country. Surprising things happen in it, of course; man and nature, unaided by Thelwell's imagination, do not often combine to produce such happy contretemps as those on pages 35 and 51. But always, as in all good farce, the background, the setting, is real, solid, convincing.

Accuracy in detail adds the pleasure of recognition to Thelwell's wildest fancies. He is not content just to draw "seagulls". Having myself an amateur interest in birds I am entranced by the overcrowded island on page 72, and have even tried to carry out a razorbill count with a magnifying glass. There are very properly, no avocets on this rocky crag, but Thelwell could not resist introducing a couple—no, three—no, I'm sorry, there are two more near the door, making five in all—into that pleasant kitchen on page 19. I am not knowledgeable about farming matters, but I do not doubt that the sheep in this book are not mere "sheep" but belong to specific breeds readily identifiable by the expert. Thelwell's popularity with country people, with the farmers and the pony-club members at whom he laughs is due to the fact that he *knows* what he is laughing at. For the rest of us, less directly attacked and ignorant, perhaps, of some of the finer points, it is enough that his ideas are so funny and he draws so well.

There is so much in this present collection to please the eye. Look at the church roof on page 26, the farm buildings on page 14, the cedar tree—and never mind the jokes for the moment—on page 23, the trawler (or is it a drifter? The uncertainty is mine, not the artist's) on page 39. Is not that a warm and grateful stackyard on page 30? It is by no means *necessary* for a humorous drawing to be in itself a pleasant thing to look at, or to be enriched by attractive detail. Much modern comic art aims at the exclusion of everything that is not intrinsic to the joke, and some highly successful and satisfying results (together with a lot of thin rubbish) have been achieved by this insistence on the utmost brevity of "statement". But humour cannot, thank goodness, be controlled by theories or confined within dogmatic limits; Thelwell's finds its proper expression "in the round"—in a recognisable world where bulls have mass and momentum, stone walls have knobbliness and texture, and combine harvesters squelch heavily through genuine mud. When a humorous artist provides visual enjoyment as well as a good laugh, I do not feel that one ought to complain.

About the quality of Thelwell's humorous ideas, as distinct from his drawing, I don't propose to argue. Humour is an individual thing, and no man will submit to being lectured on what is funny and what is not. If I were to draw the reader's attention to the drawings on pages 36, 62 and 74 as perfect examples of Thelwell's delicious, unstrained, beautifully timed humour, he would very likely draw mine to the wilder absurdities on pages 14, 51 and 95. Not that I should mind. I should be quite willing, in Round Two, to play the pony-tail joke on page 61 or the tramp on page 84 against the reader's championship of the rout of the picnickers on page 34. But I don't see where it would lead us.

There are six avocets on page 19, by the way. I quite failed to see the biggest of the lot—in flight up there under the beams.   H. F. ELLIS

thelwell country

"It's in the Green Belt, of course."

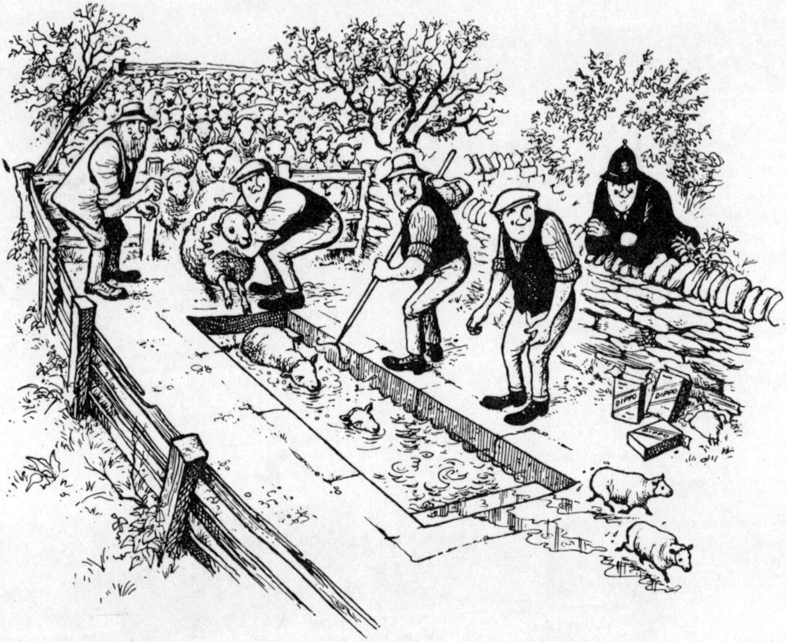
DIPPO
DIPPO
DIPPO

"There you are! Fifty per cent nylon."

"Lot 64. What am I bid?"

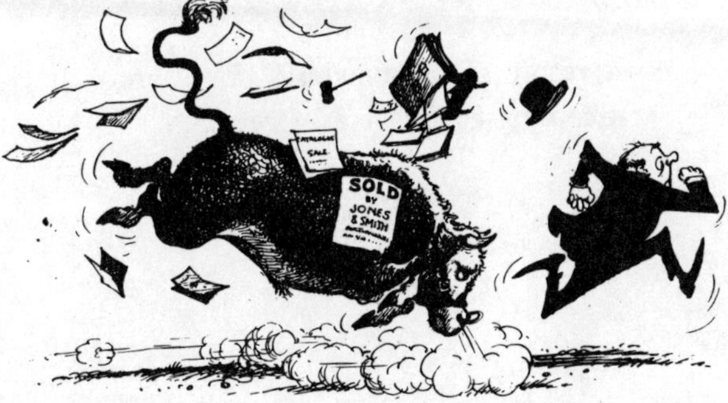
SOLD
BY
JONES
& SMITH
SALE

As a result of myxomatosis, foxes are becoming as savage as wolves . . .

and birds, owing to the Protection of Birds Act, are losing their fear of man; so that . . .

before long, life in the countryside . . .

seems likely to become complicated.

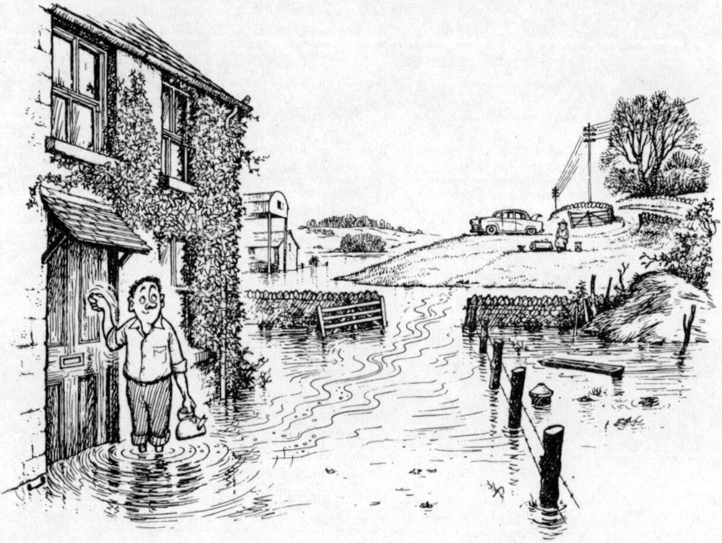

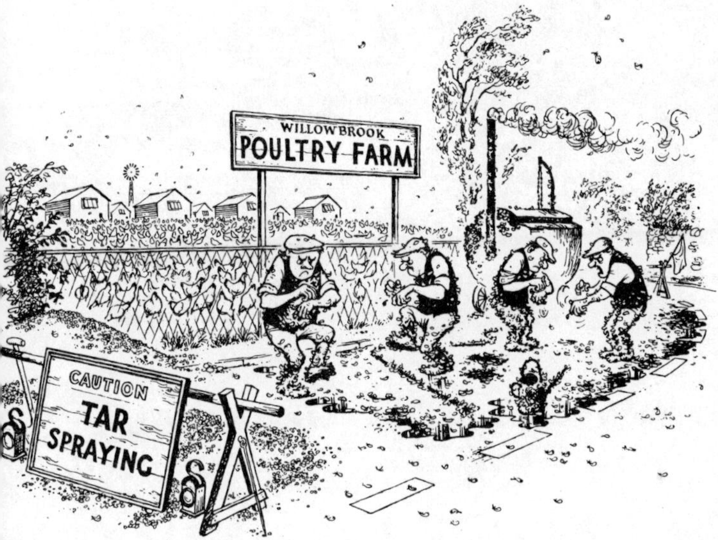
WILLOWBROOK
POULTRY FARM
CAUTION
TAR
SPRAYING

"I thought the recession wasn't supposed to affect us?"

"If we don't sell some of our surplus coal stocks soon—we'll have to consider throwing the place open to the public."

" Vicar says can you let 'im 'ave a nice bit of wheat . . .

". . . for the 'Arvest Festival?"

"On account of the widespread floods we will omit the verse about soft refreshing rain"

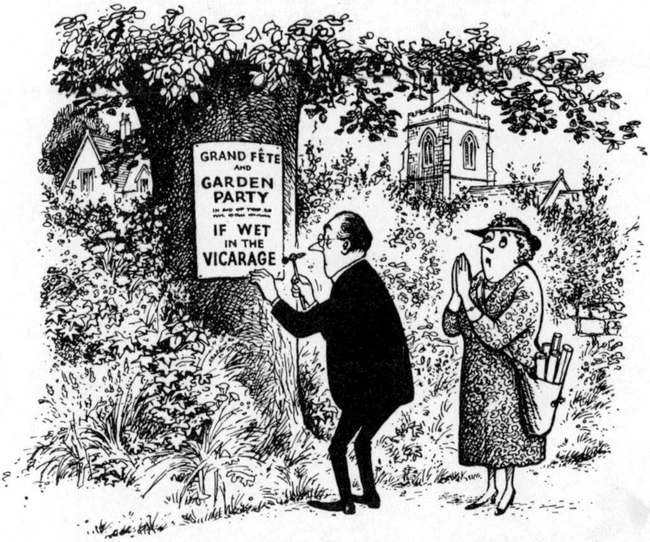
GRAND FÊTE
AND
GARDEN
PARTY
IF WET
IN THE
VICARAGE

I said "If you want a job doing properly, you've got to do it yourself."

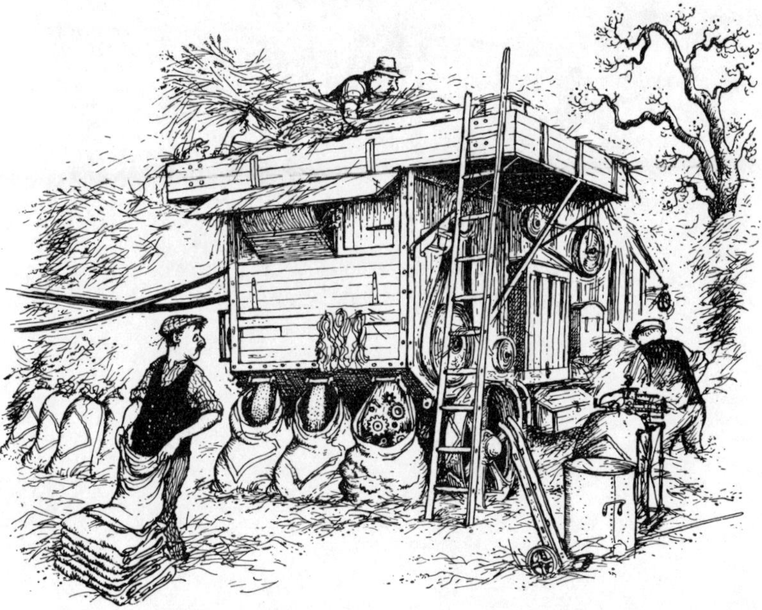

"It'll be the most disastrous year I've ever known if this lot catches fire."

"My wife's just the same. Now she wants a spin dryer."

" Quick Chaps! . . . .

. . . . . Here comes the British Travel Association Photographer."

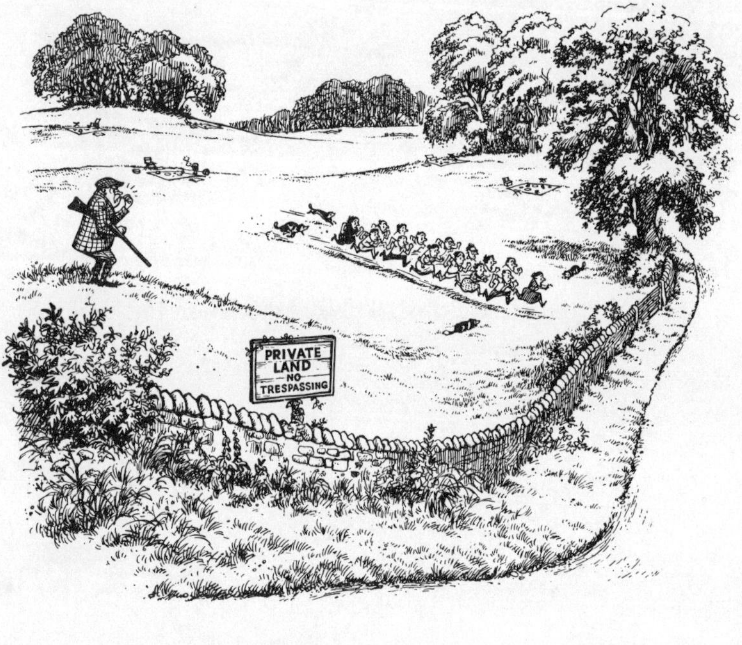
PRIVATE
LAND
NO
TRESPASSING

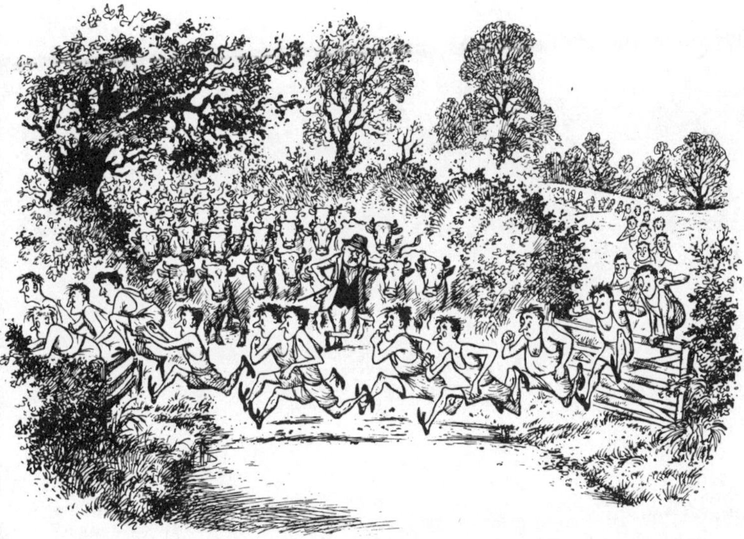

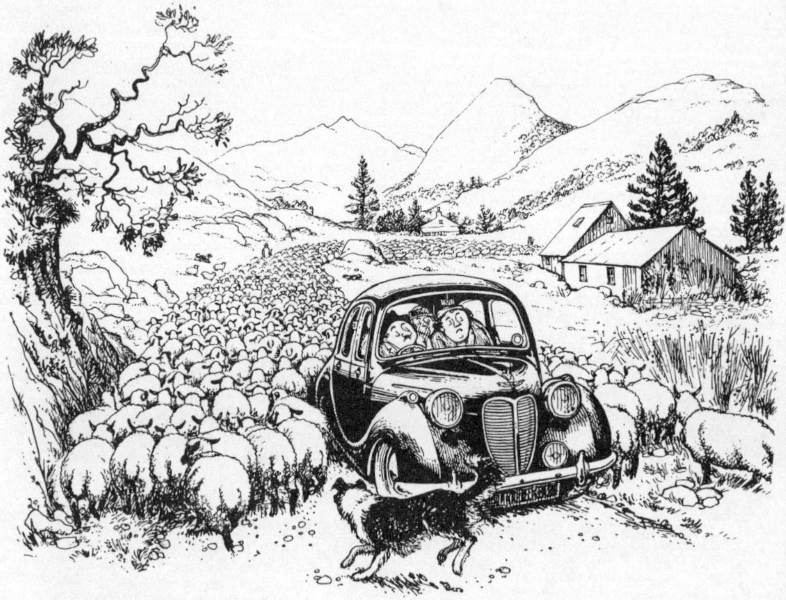

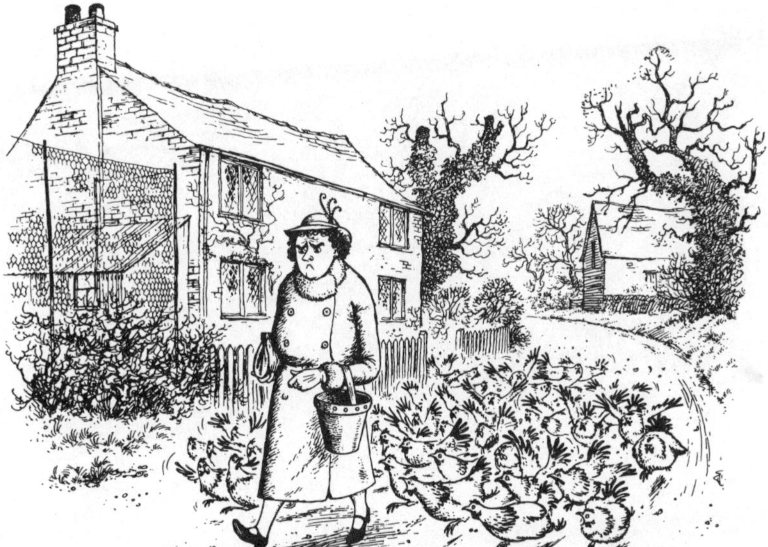

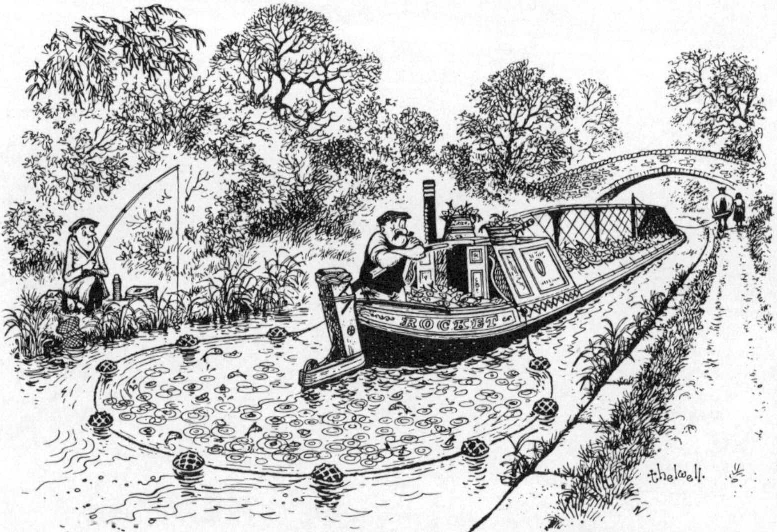
ROCKET
thelwell

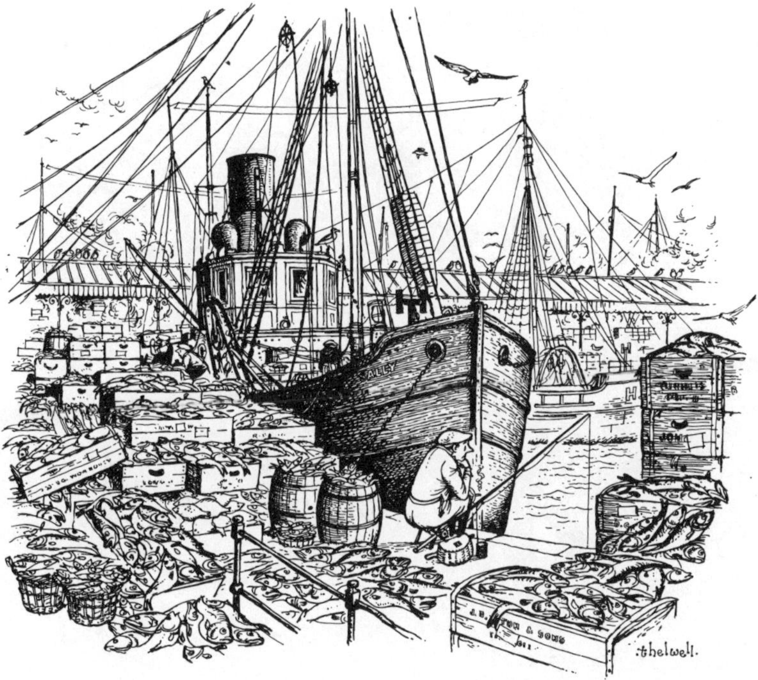

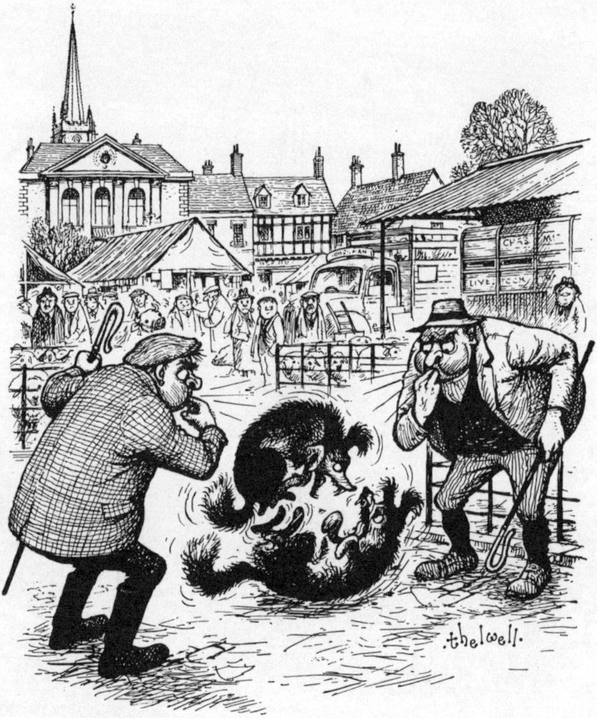
thelwell

"Know why they put glass bottoms in tankards son?"

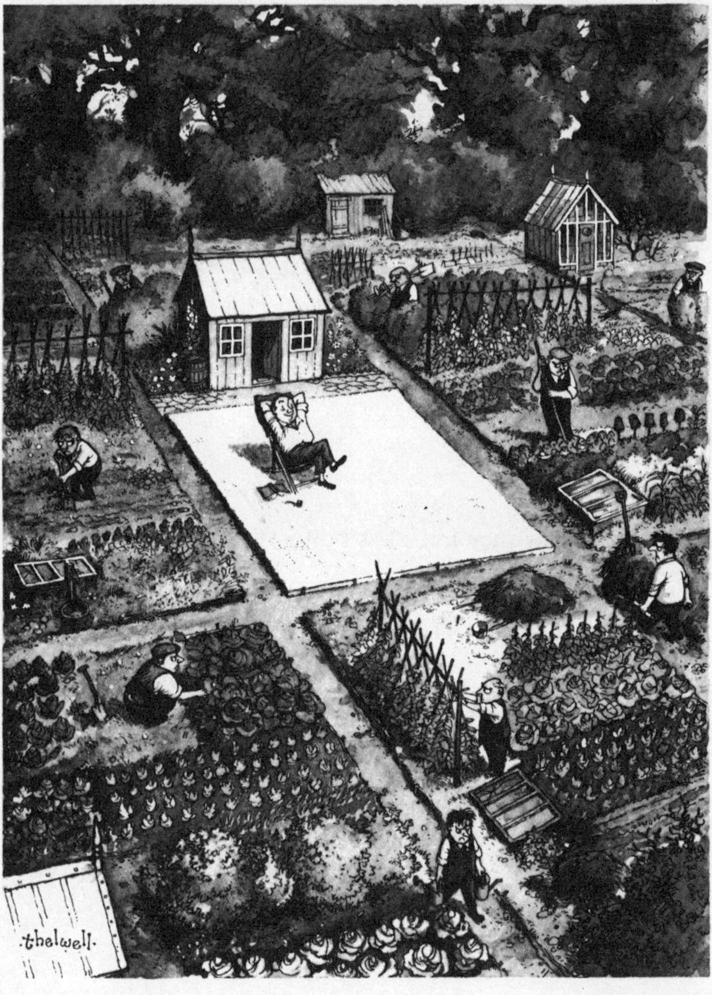
thelwell

its horses

"It's so sordid Charles—having to meet like this."

" The trouble with you city dwellers is that you just don't understand the farmers' . . .

... point of view."

The Body Beautiful
WHAT THREE MONTHS RIDING CAN DO

Before—

The Body Beautiful
WHAT THREE MONTHS RIDING CAN DO

—After

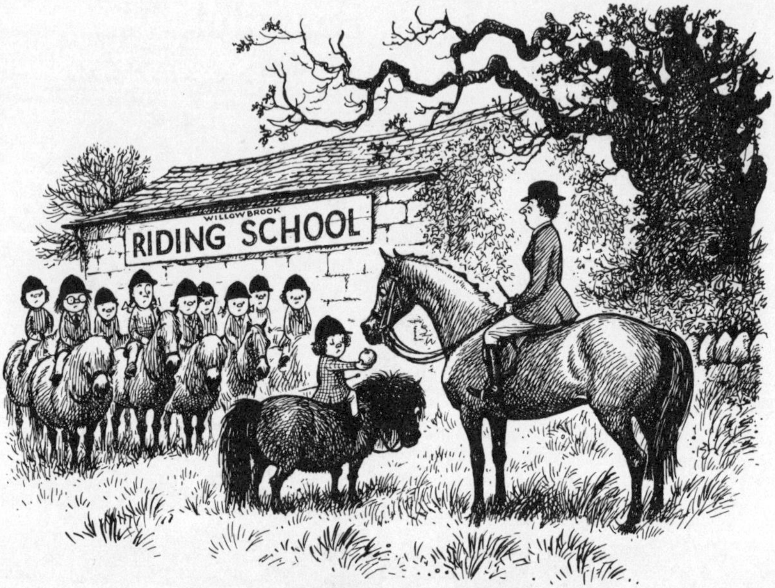
WILLOWBROOK
RIDING SCHOOL

" It's no use making a noise like that!
You've *been* blooded once."

Humane Meet

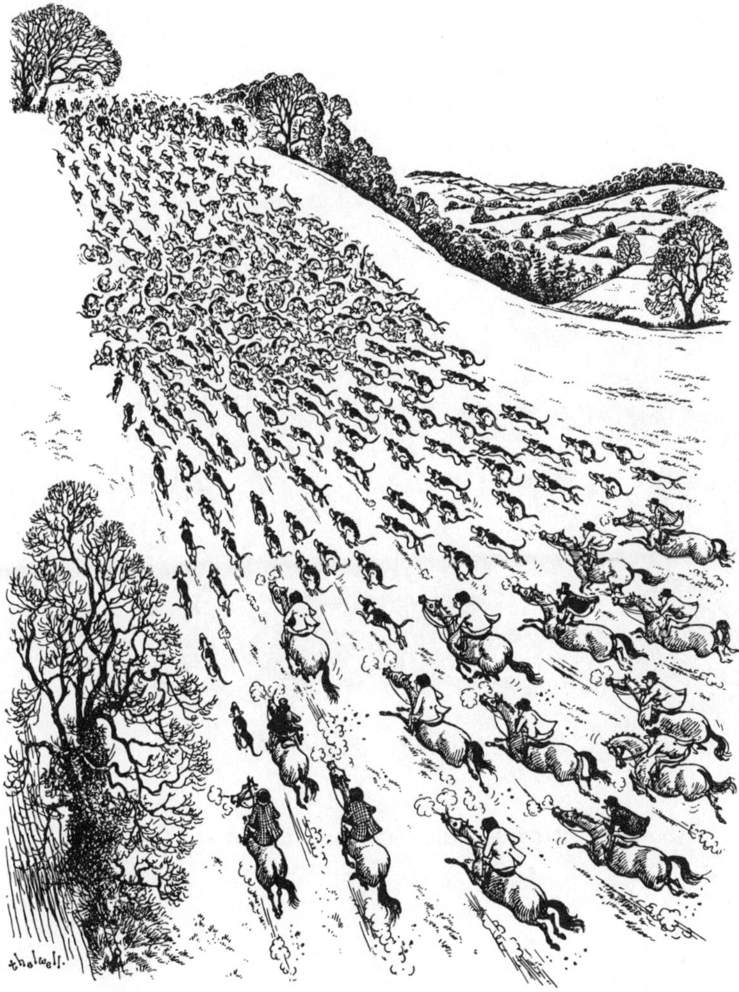
thelwell.

"Go ahead! Now tell me *that's* not the Horse of the Year!"

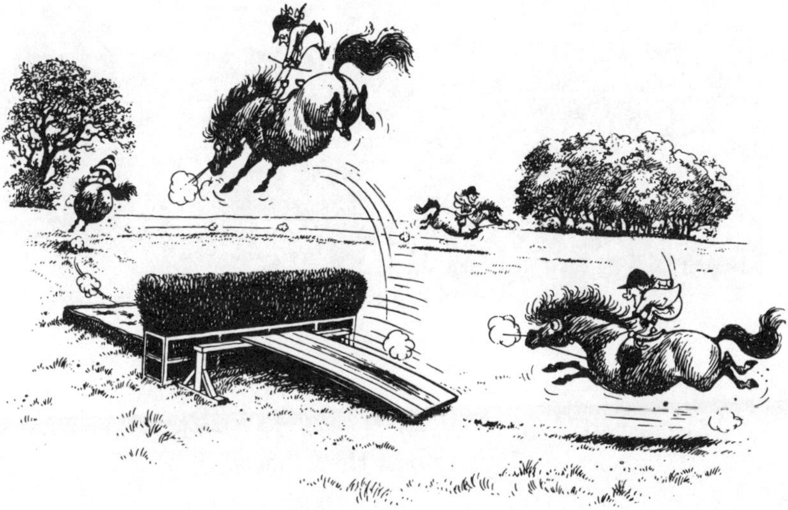

"She just asked me if she could have a few friends in to watch the International Horse Show."

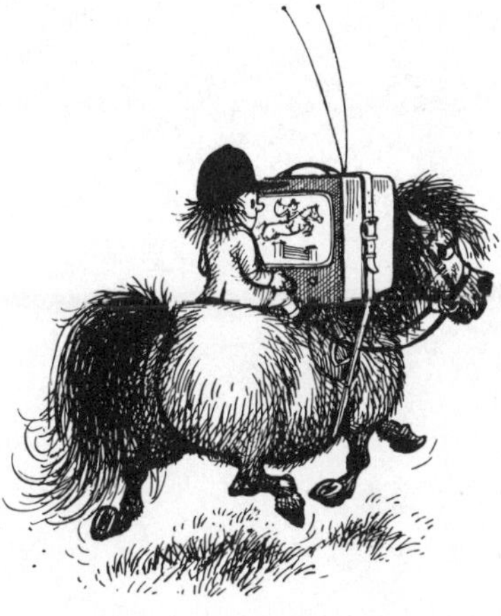

"I'll just try to get him to say a few words."

"Here comes Charlie! Let's have a rubber of bridge."

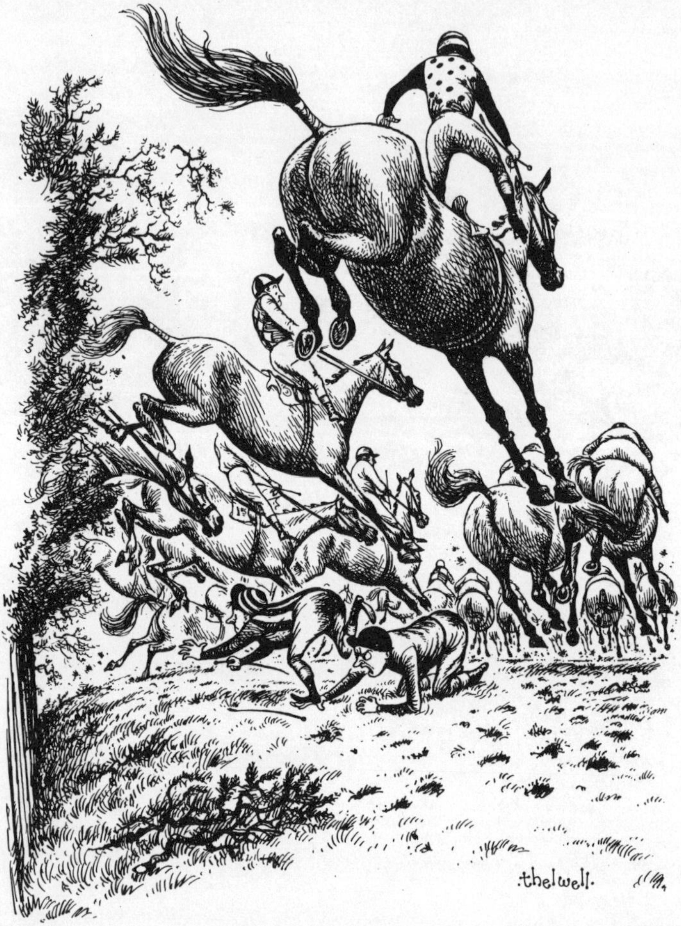
thelwell

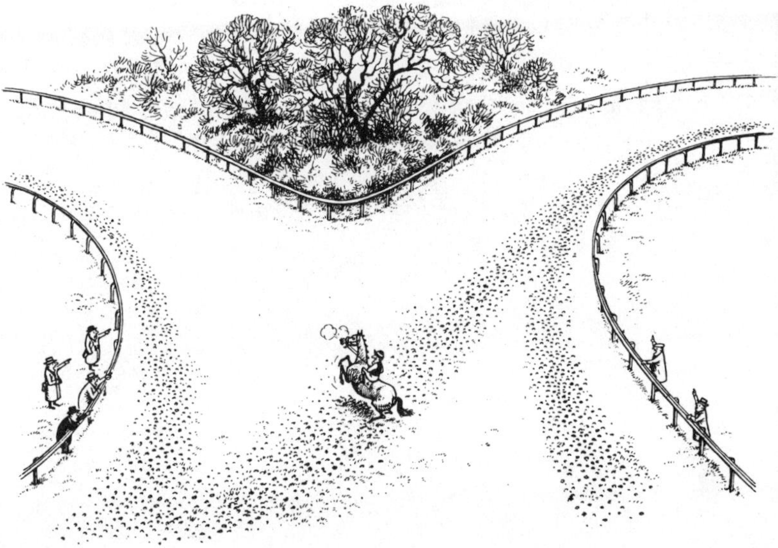

"Now we mustn't lose our temper Wendy. Perhaps we'll be good enough for the gymkhana next year."

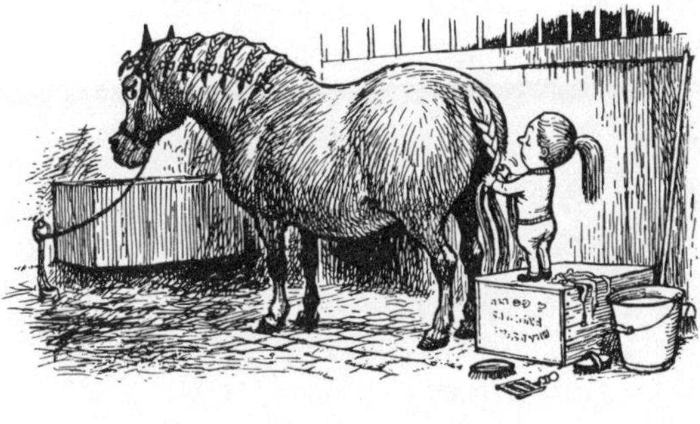

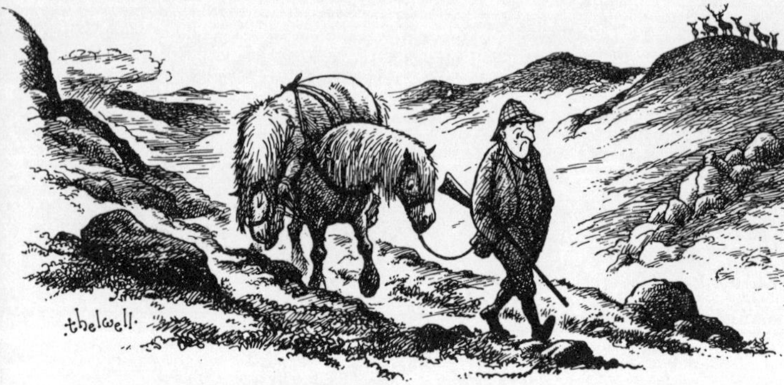
thelwell

its bird life

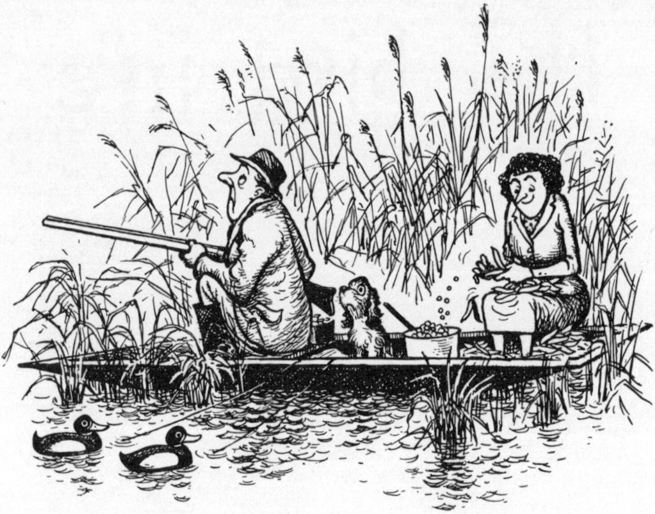

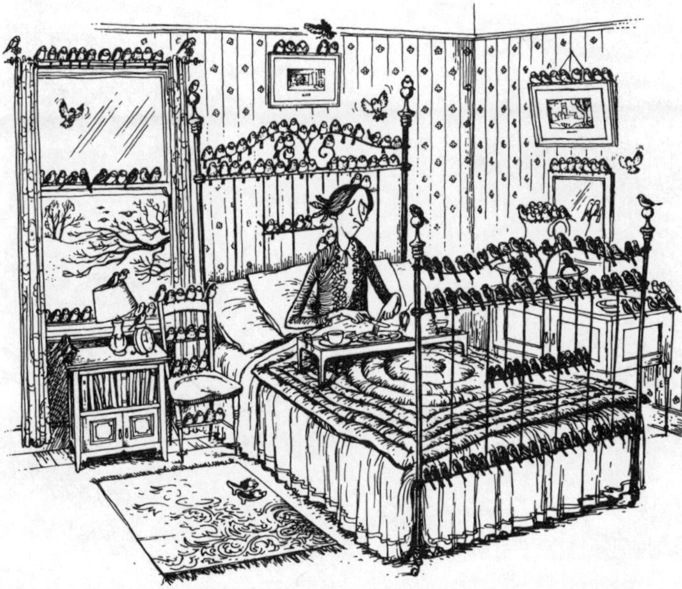

"All right Charlie! Send them up."

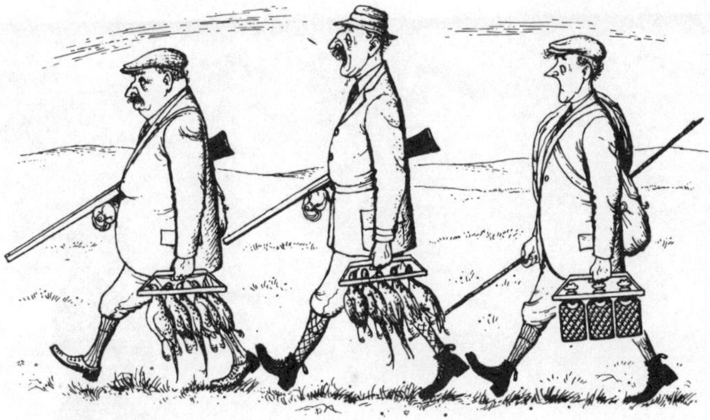

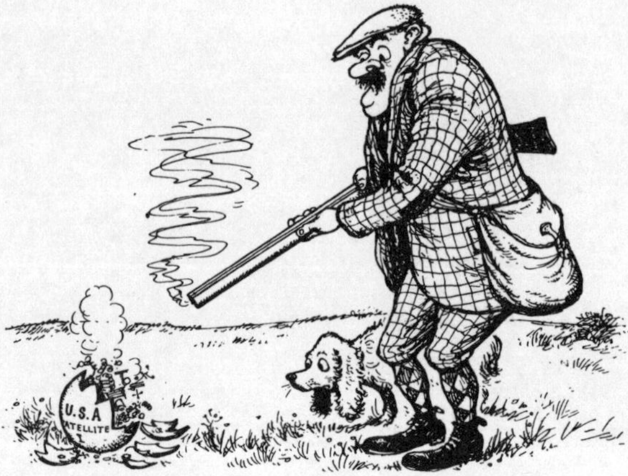
U.S.A
ATELLITE
I

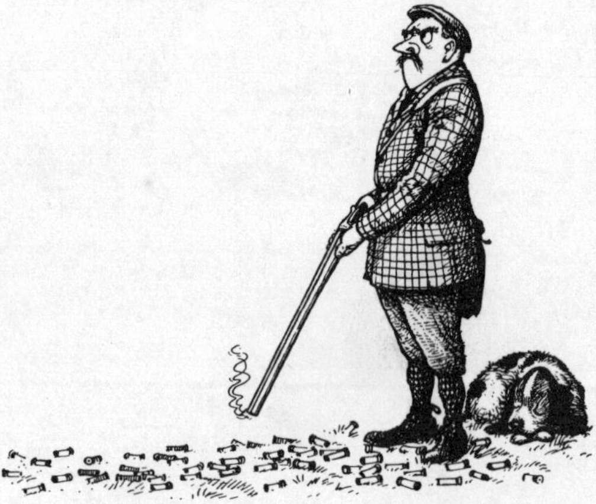

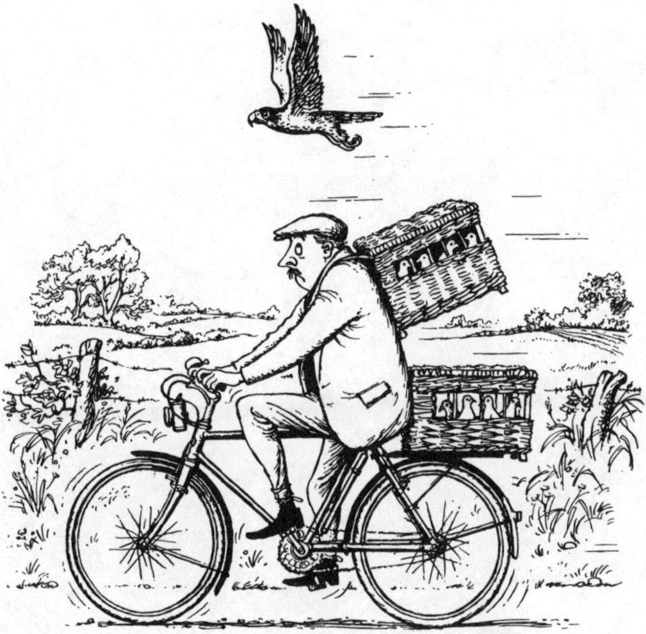

"I warned you against fish paste sandwiches."

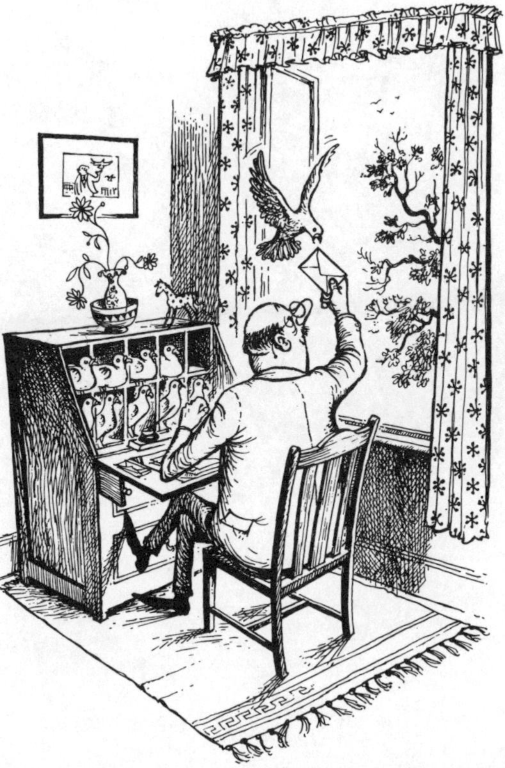

"Where do we set up the hide?"

73

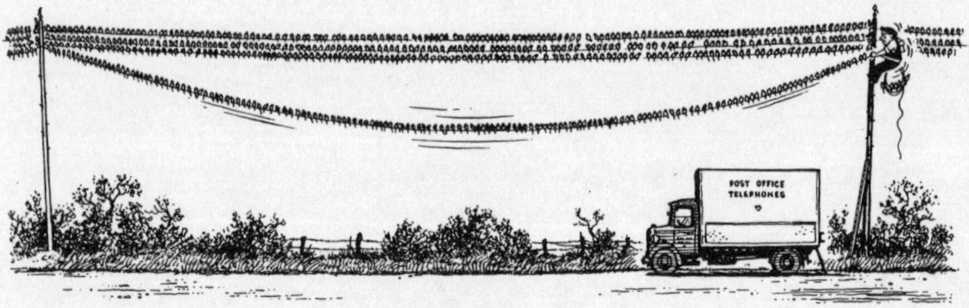
POST OFFICE
TELEPHONES

its nomads

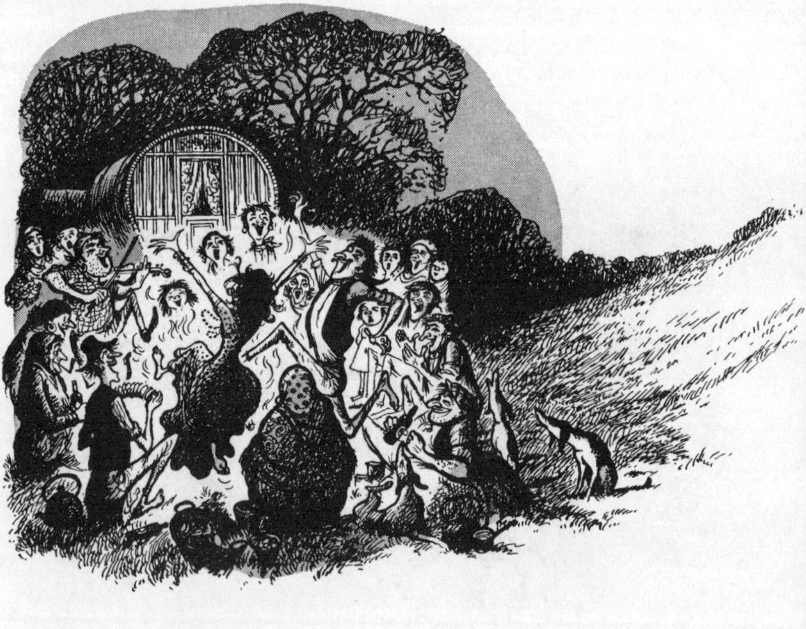

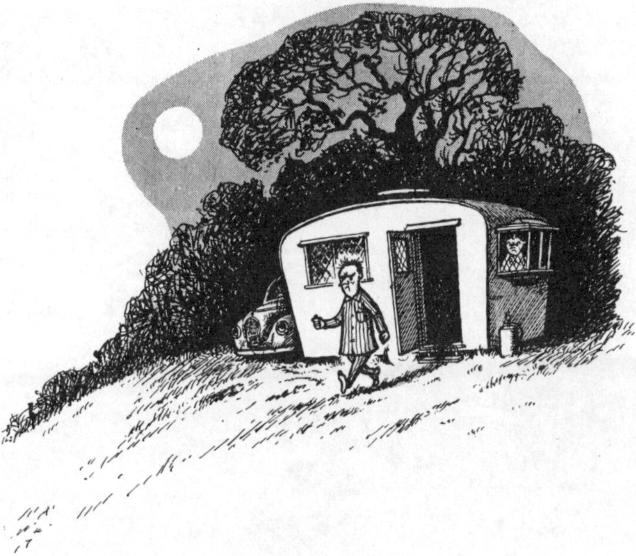

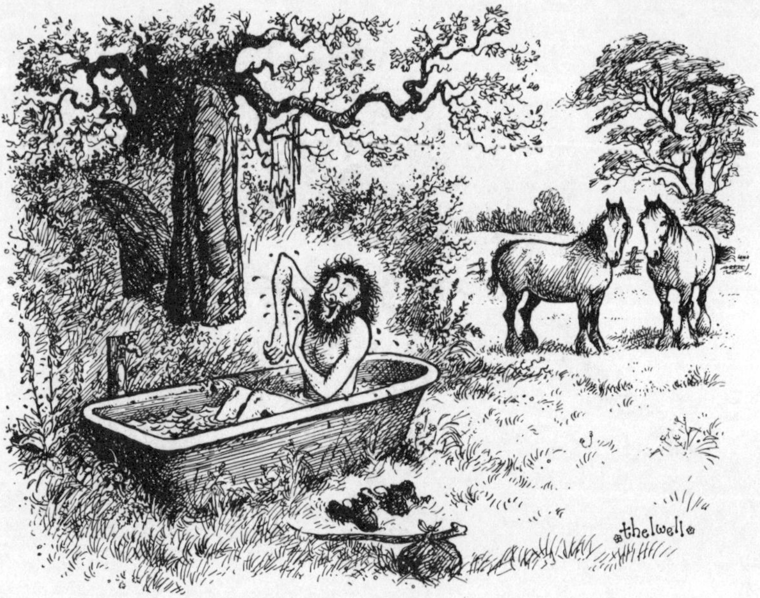
thelwell

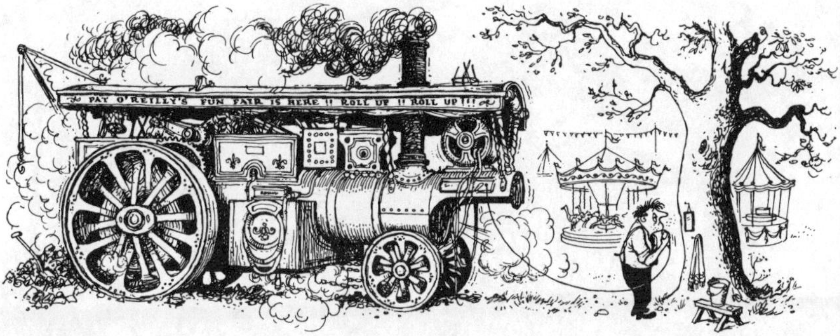
PAT O'REILLY'S FUN FAIR IS HERE !! ROLL UP !! ROLL UP !!!

"It's their simplicity that I envy."

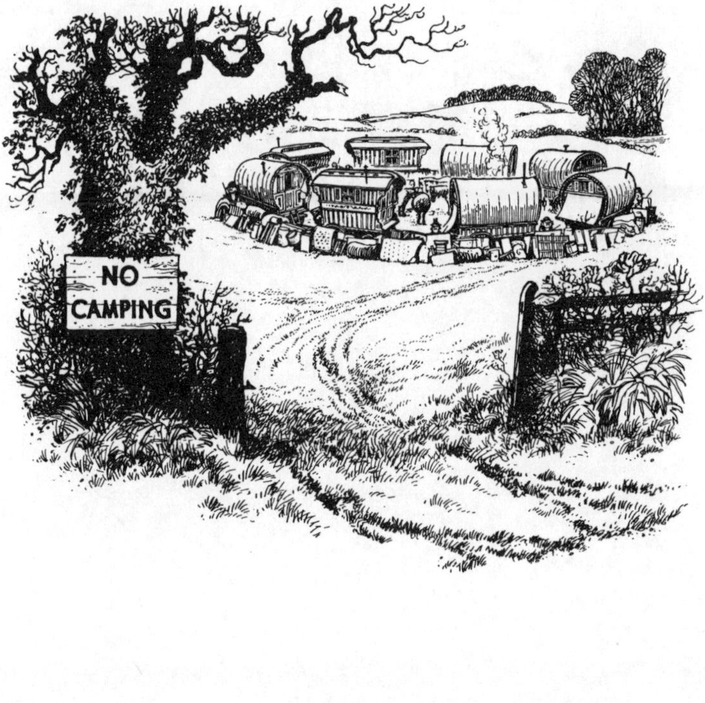
NO
CAMPING

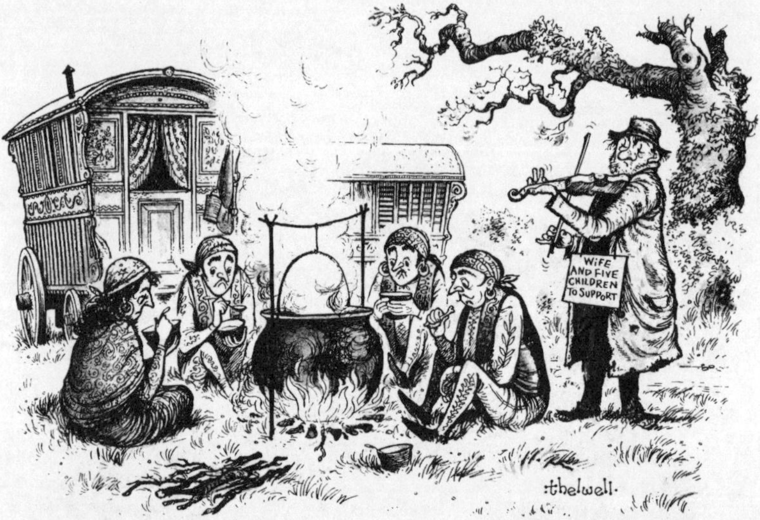
WIFE
AND FIVE
CHILDREN
TO SUPPORT
thelwell

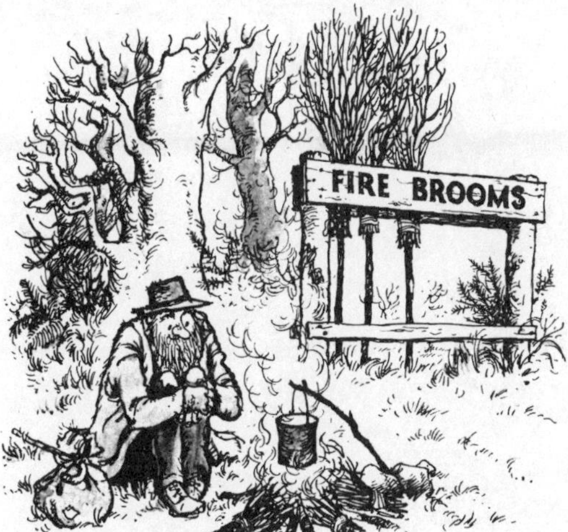
FIRE BROOMS
thelwell

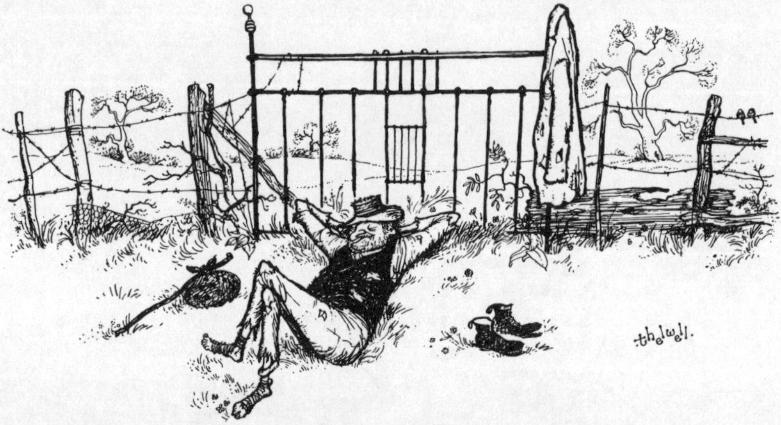
thelwell.

its trade

" It's nice to see that modern sales techniques have at last . . . .

"... reached our village."

Universal Pet Stores
MEATOMEAL
GREEN
Confectioner
SCATTS
DOGS LOVE 'EM

PETS CORNER
EVERYTHING MUST GO!
SLEEKAT for WORM
BONES THE FOOD FOR DOGS

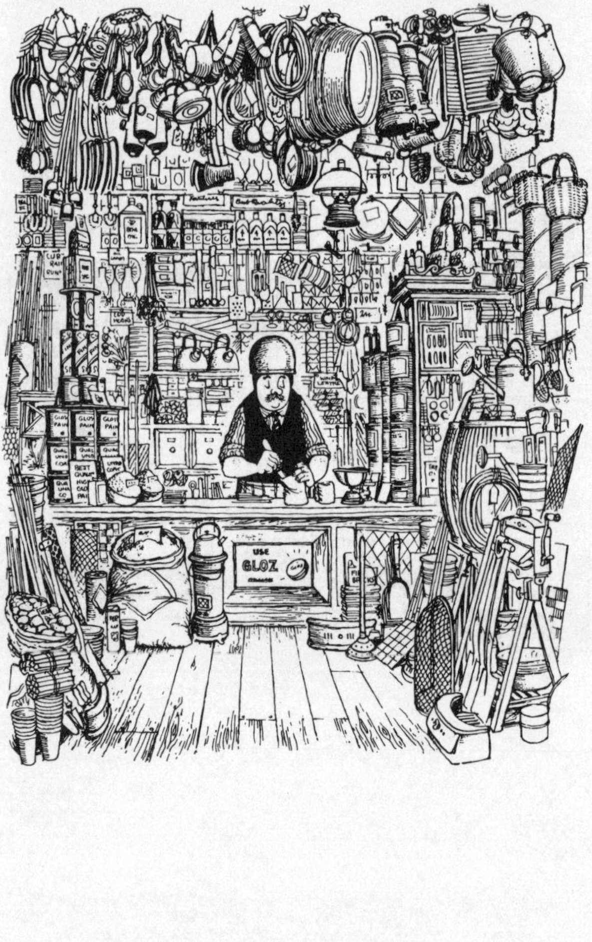
USE
GLOZ

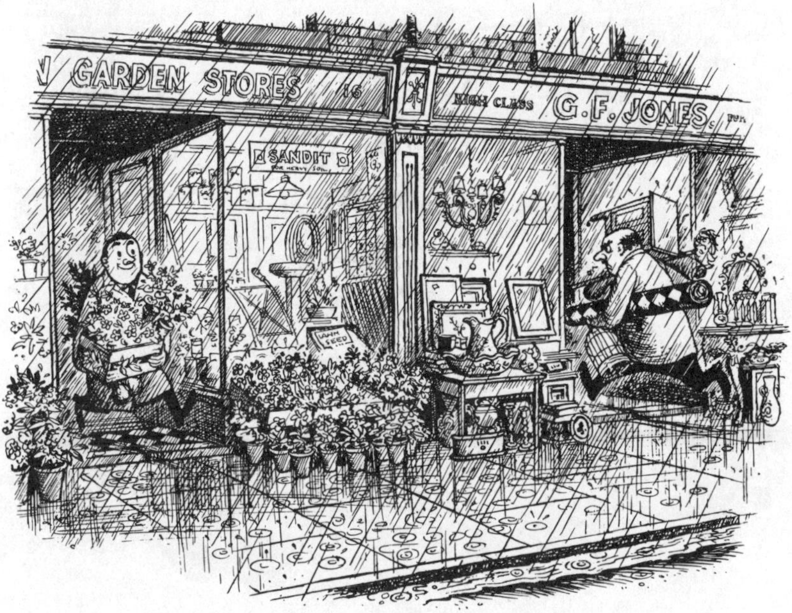
GARDEN STORES
16
SANDIT
HIGH CLASS
G.F. JONES
LAWN SEED

TABBY
DOG AND CAT MEAT FRESH DAILY
THE PET SHOP
PUSS
TROPICAL FISH FOR SALE
DUSTEX
PETSO
FOR DOGS
PETSO
PETSO
BEST QUALITY

Greengrocer
BROWN'S
Fruit Merchant
UNDER NEW MANAGEMENT
AFRICAN
KING EDWARDS
IN SPAN!
ENGLISH

"Lovely firewood."

"Who's there?"

and, of course, its people

Angels on Horseback

ANGELS ON HORSEBACK

— AND ELSE-WHERE

by thelwell

New York, E. P. Dutton & Co., Inc., 1971

PRINTED IN GREAT BRITAIN

COPYRIGHT 1957 BY NORMAN THELWELL

For
DAVID & PENNY

Most of the pictures originally appeared in *Punch* and are published here by kind permission of the proprietors.

CONTENTS

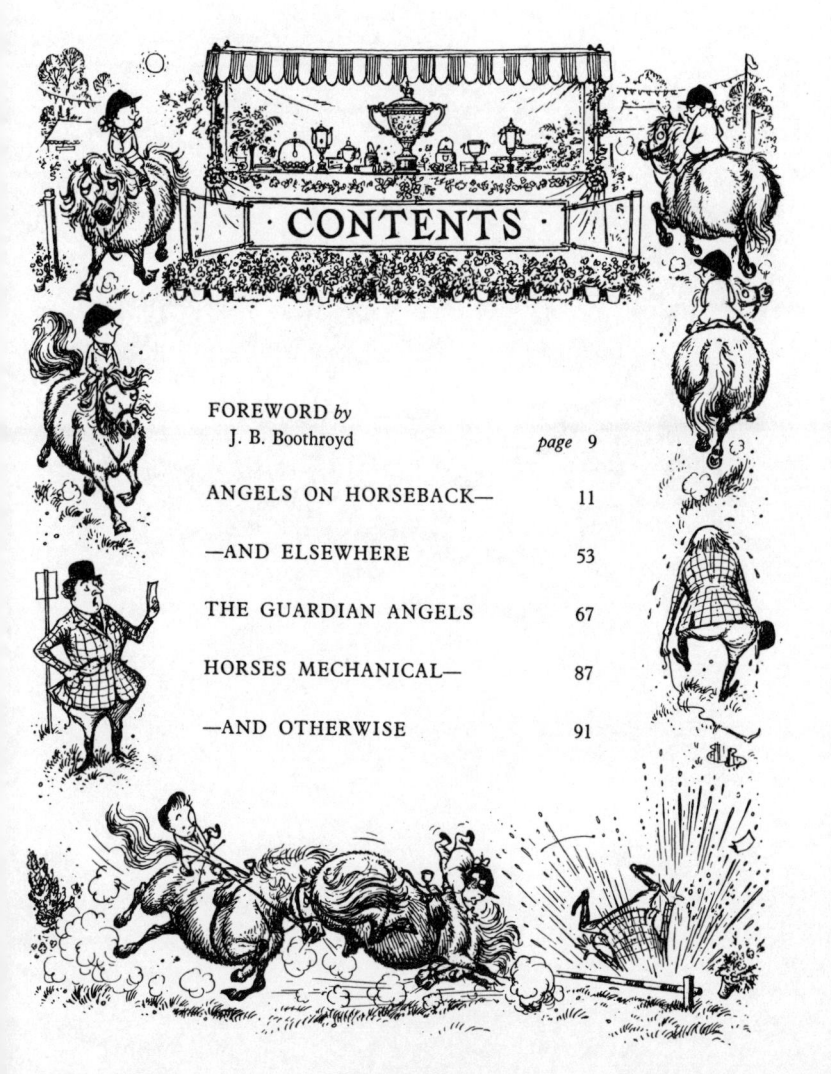

FOREWORD by J. B. Boothroyd	page 9
ANGELS ON HORSEBACK—	11
—AND ELSEWHERE	53
THE GUARDIAN ANGELS	67
HORSES MECHANICAL—	87
—AND OTHERWISE	91

"Now the fall is important."

FOREWORD

THERE was a song, 'Crazy Over Horses'. They weren't Thelwell's kind, but the kind that exist on shaved green turf for the few, the back page of the evening papers for the many—and for him nowhere. He doesn't recognize them. His horses never brought a grandstand to its feet, clashing binoculars. Brains are not blown out over them. Yet they are the horses that people who know horses know.

I do not know horses. But I have come nearer to it through these drawings than in any other way. For me they have humanized both horses and horsepeople—and if you think there is no such thing as a human horse, eavesdrop at the nearest Hunt Ball. As a lifelong non-equestrian I have suffered many a pang of inferiority, because there is something terribly crushing about anyone on a horse. Even a home-going labourer clomping past me in a country lane, side-saddle and bareback (if that can be), tempts me to touch my forelock, and astounds me by touching his first.

No doubt it's something to do with the height. The rider can't help looking down on the rest of the world, and it is easy to imagine that he is looking down his own nose as well as the horse's. However, I know at last that is not so. Thelwell has convinced me, and I can never be too grateful, that the horse person is, if possible, even less sure of himself than I am. Even those russet-coloured lumps on horses' backs that prove, as they jog into focus, to be small children in tiny velvet caps and impeccable little Jodhpurs which they must be literally growing out of every second, hold no terrors for me now. They are revealed as palpitating bundles of exposed nerve-ends, liable to be shot through a blackthorn hedge any minute like a stone from a catapult. This comforts me. In future, instead of avoiding the eye of middle-aged ladies with bowler hats and Roman noses who gallop at me round the blind corners of Sussex byways, I shall watch them keenly out of sight. Thelwell may have a disaster arranged for them.

Punch has had equestrian artists before. In mid-Victorian times it was difficult to open a copy without being trampled. But the creations between these present covers achieve something entirely new: they combine portraiture with caricature, a thing which most artists would hesitate to try with human beings, let alone the more temperamentally elusive and psychologically inscrutable horse. This means that while no horse could possibly look exactly like a Thelwell horse, all Thelwell horses manage to look exactly like horses. If anyone can explain this, or express it more lucidly, they should write to the publishers, please, not me.

To end with a reminder that Thelwell is not only an artist but a humorist is not to suggest that anyone could overlook it, but to make it clear that I haven't. It is hard for one practising humorist to praise another . . . but how is it that all these centuries have gone by without anyone thinking of the joke on page 51? Or 60? Or, for that matter ——?

But, anyway, they're all yours now.

J. B. Boothroyd

Angels on Horseback

Booted and Spurned
A GUIDE TO BRITISH PONY BREEDS

1. *DARTMOOR AND EXMOOR*
Though inclined to be wild—these ponies make lovable mounts if taken from the moors early enough.

2. *CONNEMARA.* Mostly grey nowadays—are among the oldest inhabitants of the British Isles.

3. *NEW FOREST.* Due to the abundance of traffic in the area—this rather narrow breed is said to be immune to the terror of modern roads.

4. *WELSH MOUNTAIN*
Perhaps the most beautiful of our native ponies but it is debatable whether the 'dished' face line is due to Arab influence.

5. *FELL AND DALE.* Originally used to carry lead—are ideal for the larger family.

6. *HIGHLAND.* The largest and strongest and quite unrivalled in surefootedness.

7. *SHETLAND.* The smallest and hardiest breed of all and perfect for introducing children to the problems of horsemanship.

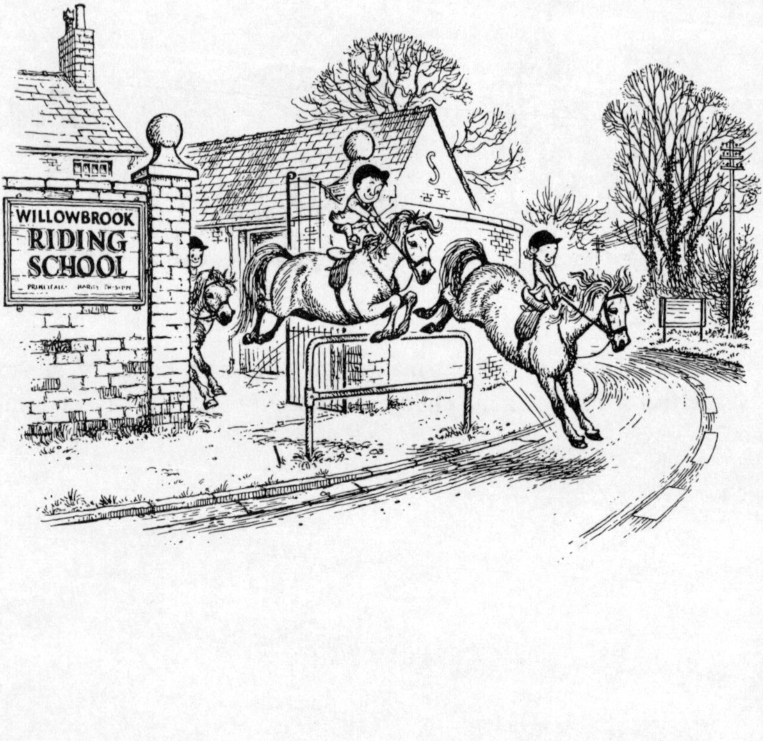
WILLOWBROOK
RIDING
SCHOOL

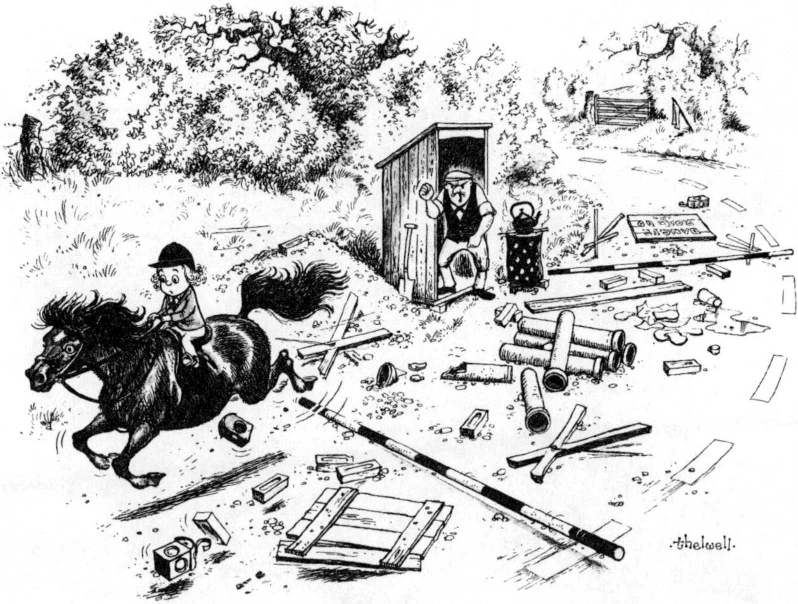
thelwell

" 'ow do *they* feel then?"

"I see you've kicked the toes out of them already."

Small in the Saddle
A FEW POINTERS WHEN BUYING A PONY

1. A child regards his first pony as a new plaything.

2. They must suit each other in temperament

3. Experience is needed when buying from public auctions

4. It is not always easy to recognise a good pony "in the rough".

5. The mount should not be too wide for the child's short legs.

6. Daily exercise is most important

7. And careful grooming
essential to the pony's happiness

Anyway, it's a wonderful way for a child to learn how to enjoy Man's mastery over nature.

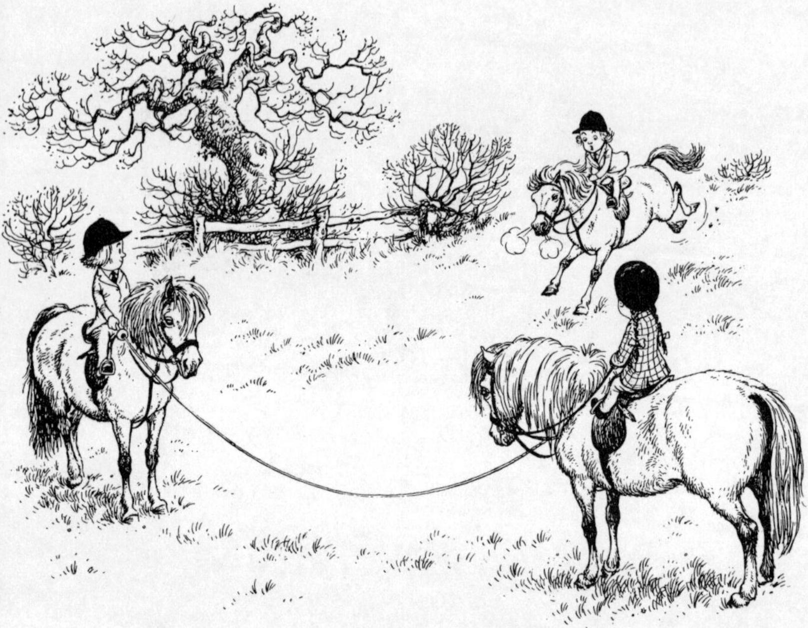

Look before you Leap
A CHILD'S GUIDE TO SHOW-JUMPING

The opportunity to examine the fences before the start of the competition should never be missed.

The signal to start is given by a bell, flag or whistle.

Look before you Leap
A CHILD'S GUIDE TO SHOW-JUMPING

A horse or pony is said to have "REFUSED" if he stops in front of a fence...

...and to have "FALLEN" if the shoulders and quarters have touched the ground.

Look before you Leap
A CHILD'S GUIDE TO SHOW-JUMPING

A competitor is eliminated for showing any fence to a horse after a refusal.

Or for unauthorised assistance whether solicited or not.

Look before you Leap
A CHILD'S GUIDE TO SHOW-JUMPING

Endless patience is required to reach perfection.

But for those who ultimately achieve a clear round—the rewards are many.

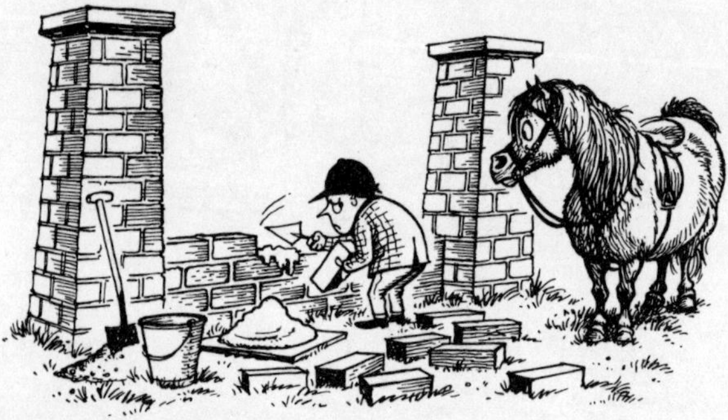

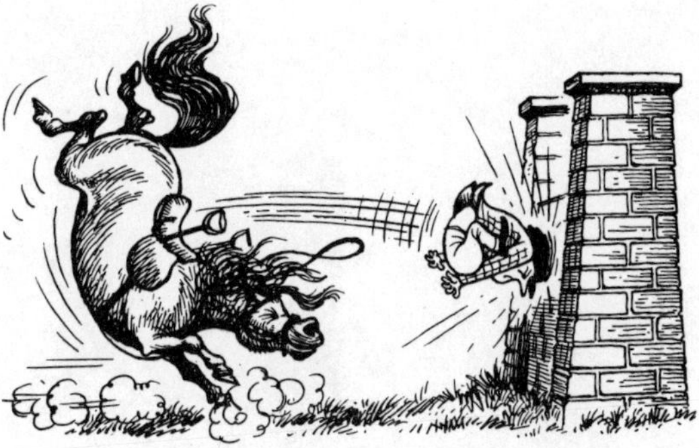

Horse Show
AT THE WHITE CITY

Miss Pam Smith on the famous " Tusker " enters the arena.

Willowbrook Show
ON THE GREEN

Shirley Wilkinson and " Tearaway " enter the ring.

Horse Show
AT THE WHITE CITY

Mr. Robinson's "Firebird" taking the water.

Willowbrook Show
ON THE GREEN

Tom Jenkins' " Thistledown " taking the water.

Horse Show
AT THE WHITE CITY

Col. Boyce-Partington on "Prince Consort" at the wall.

Willowbrook Show
ON THE GREEN

Four-year-old Penelope Bright riding "Nimble" tackles an obstacle.

Horse Show
AT THE WHITE CITY

The Marquis of Basingstoke presented the trophies.

Willowbrook Show
ON THE GREEN

"Well jumped Mary", laughed Mrs. Hornby-James who presented the prizes.

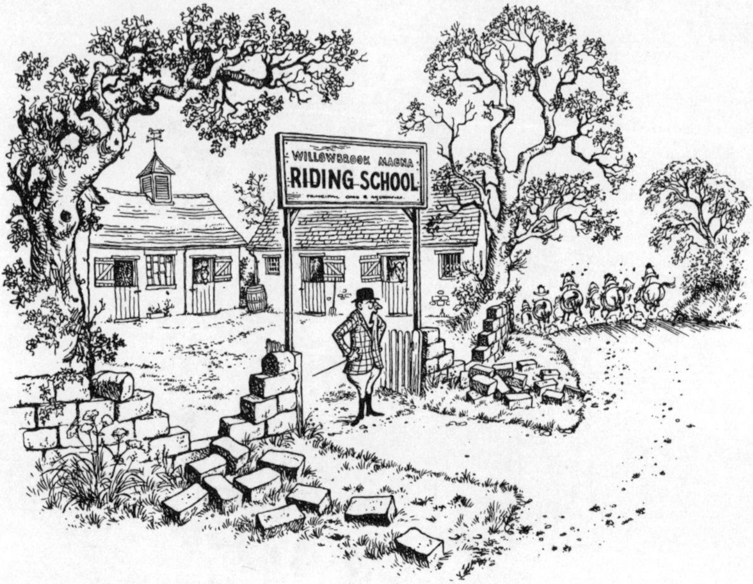
WILLOWBROOK MAGNA
RIDING SCHOOL

42

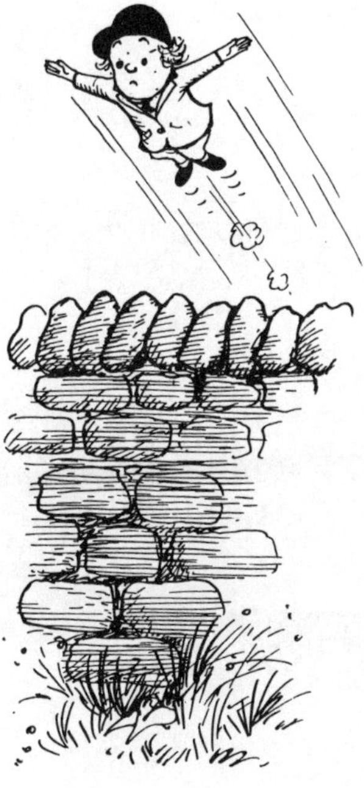

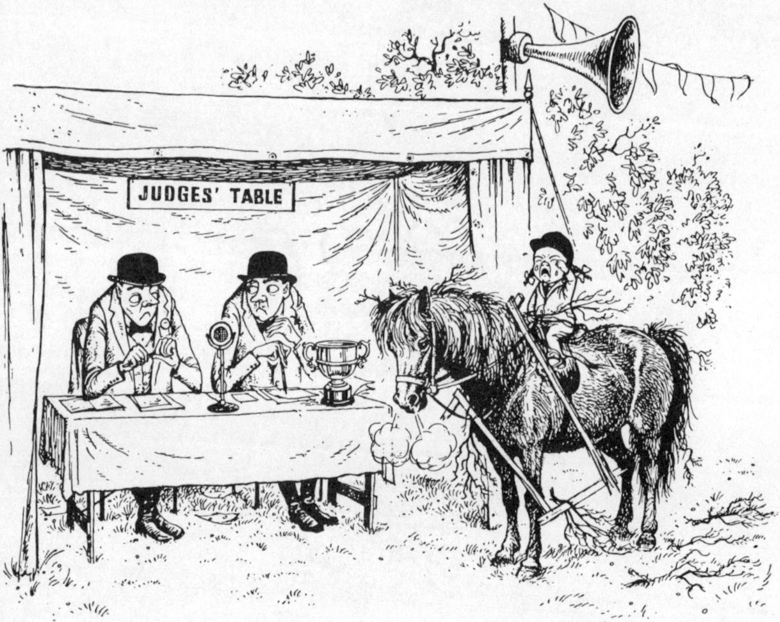
JUDGES' TABLE

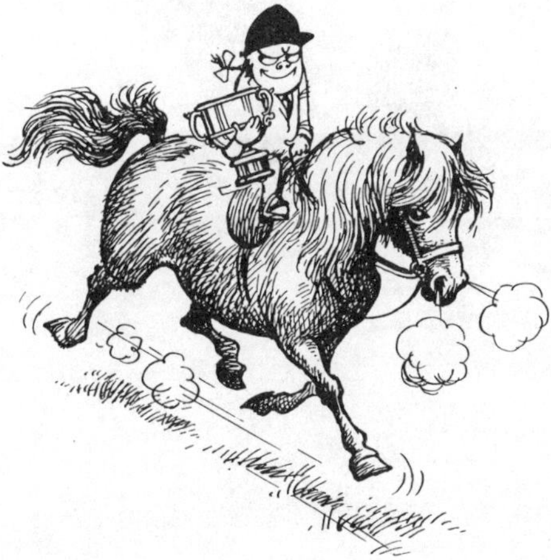

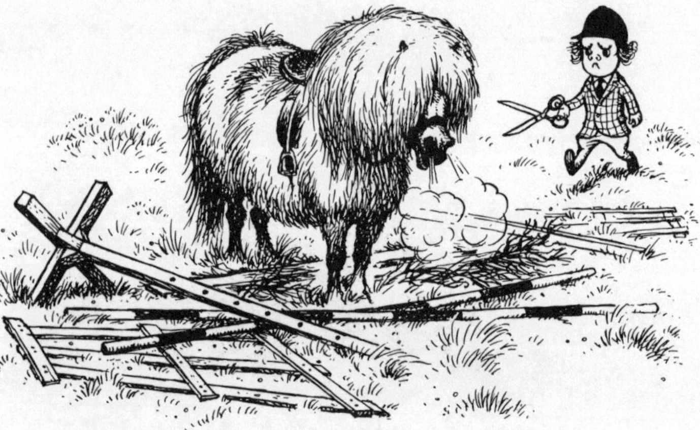

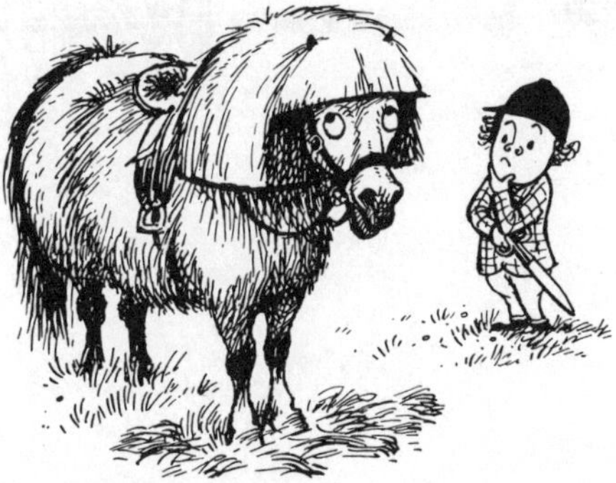

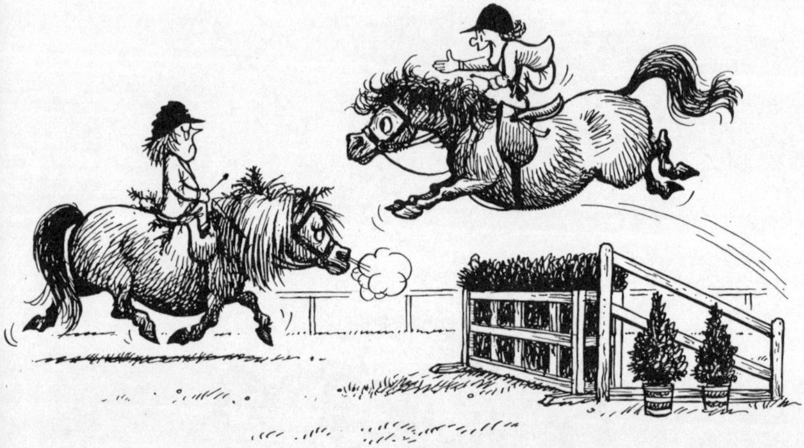

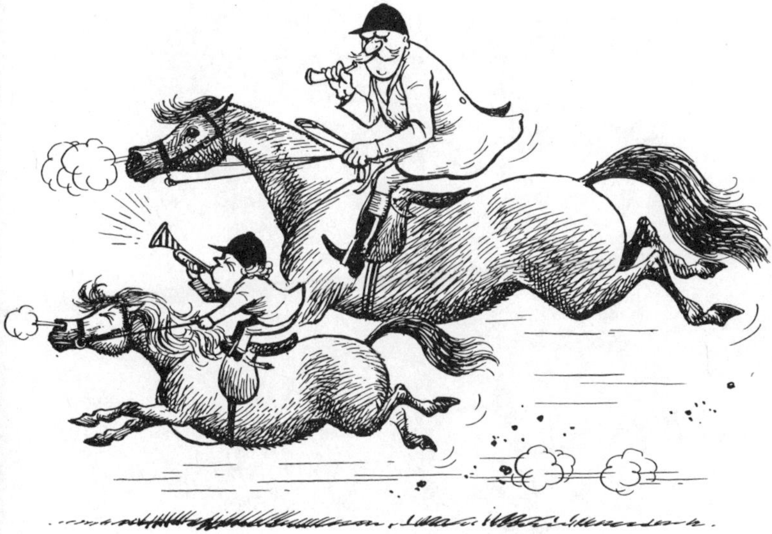

"I'm sorry I ever mentioned he'd got a stone in his hoof."

"HEEL!"

–And Elsewhere

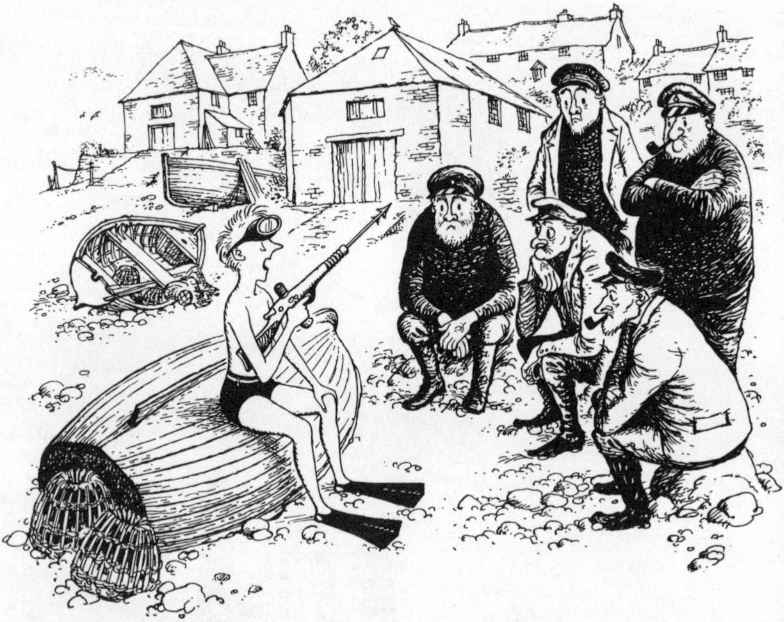

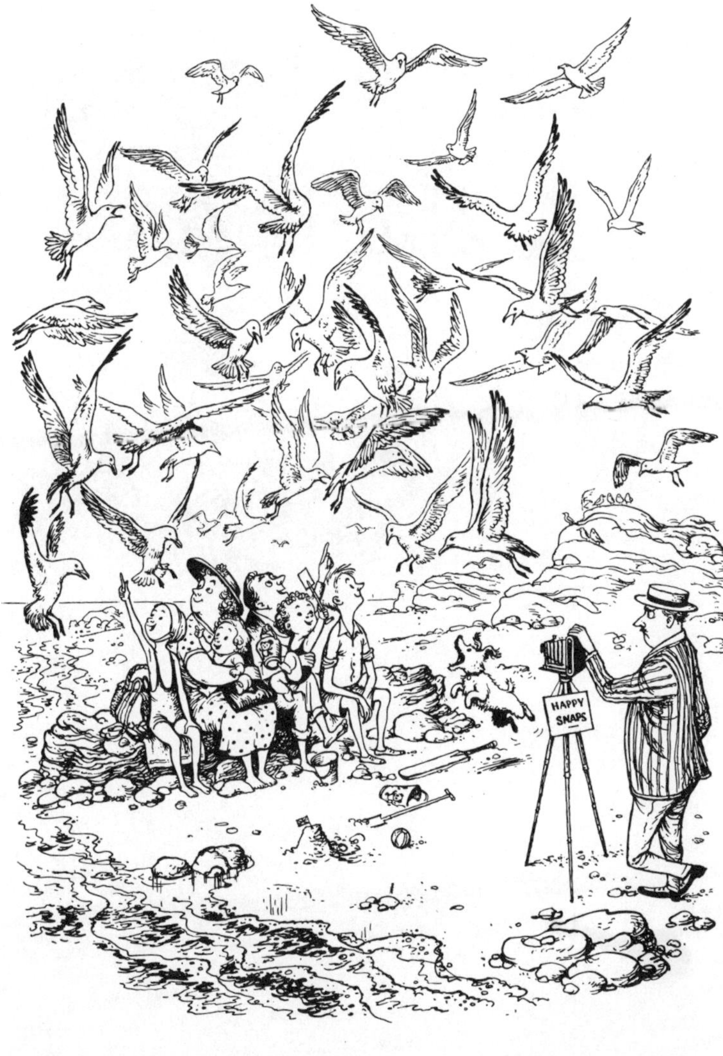
HAPPY
SNAPS

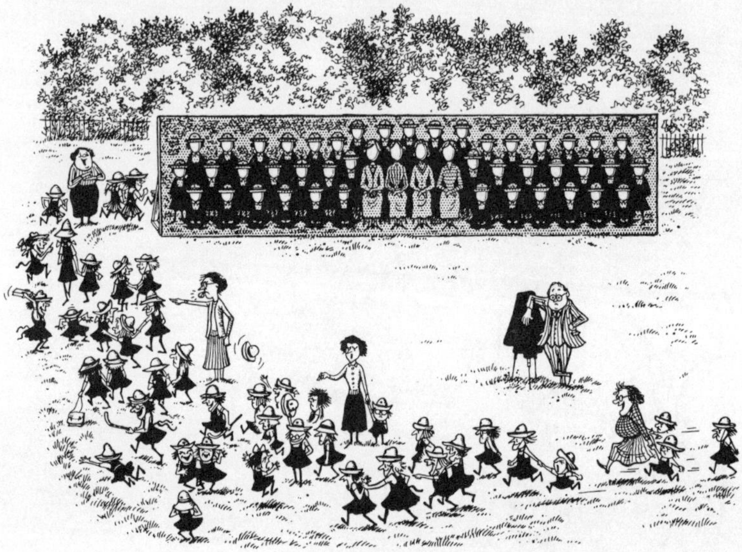

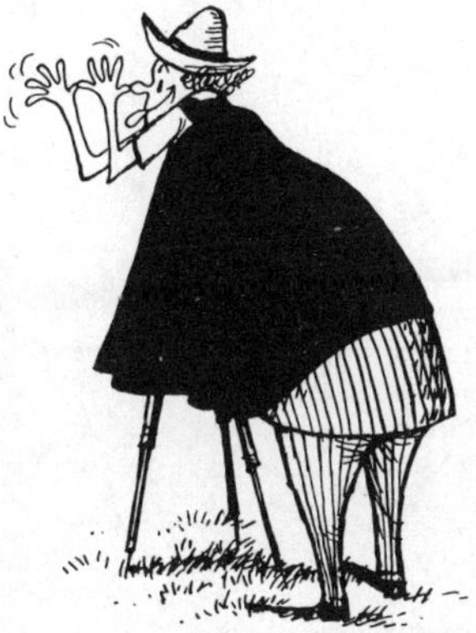

"What have I told you about drawing on the walls?"

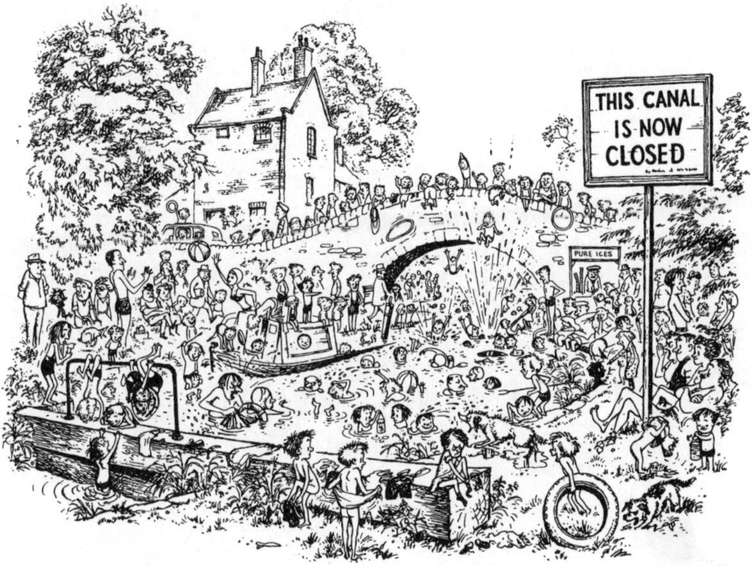
THIS CANAL IS NOW CLOSED
PURE ICES

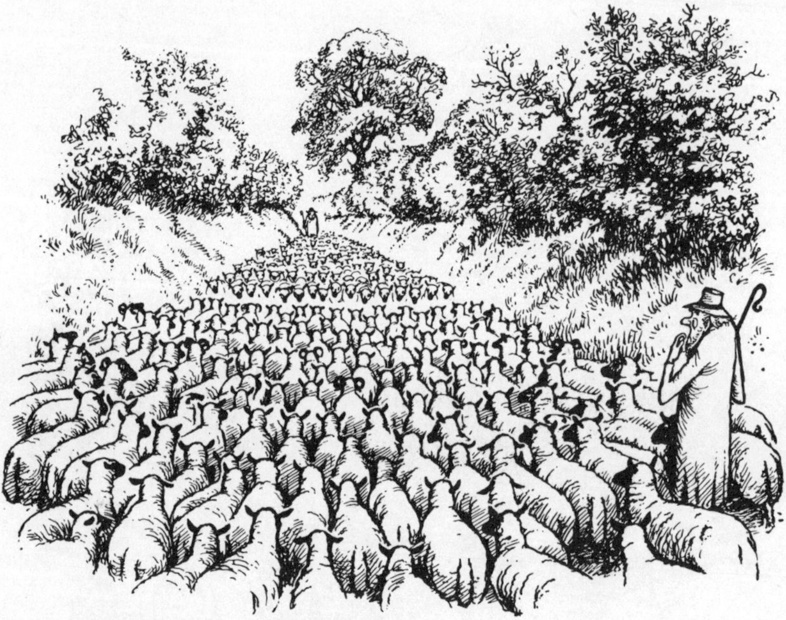

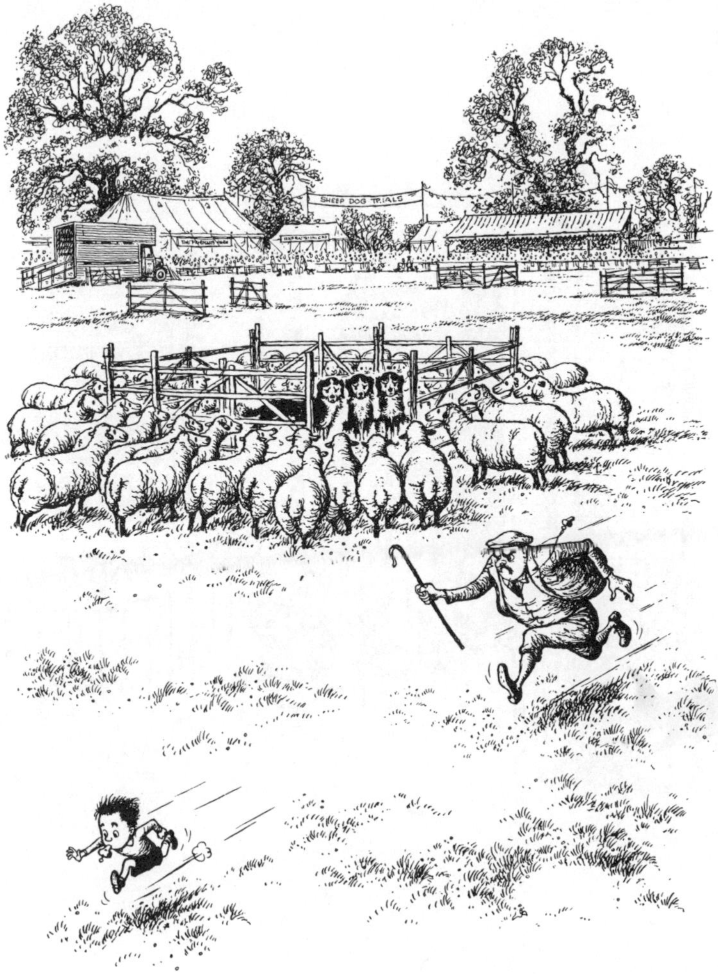
SHEEP DOG TRIALS

"You rang?"

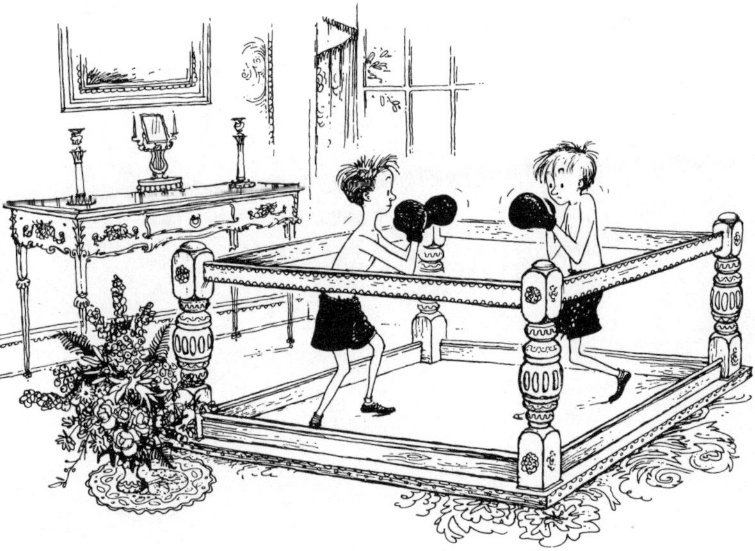

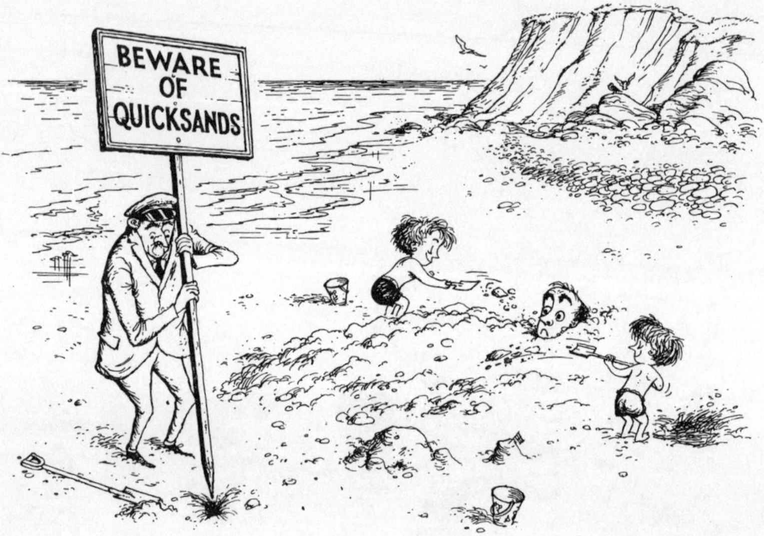
BEWARE
OF
QUICKSANDS

". . . and hurry . . ."

The Guardian Angels

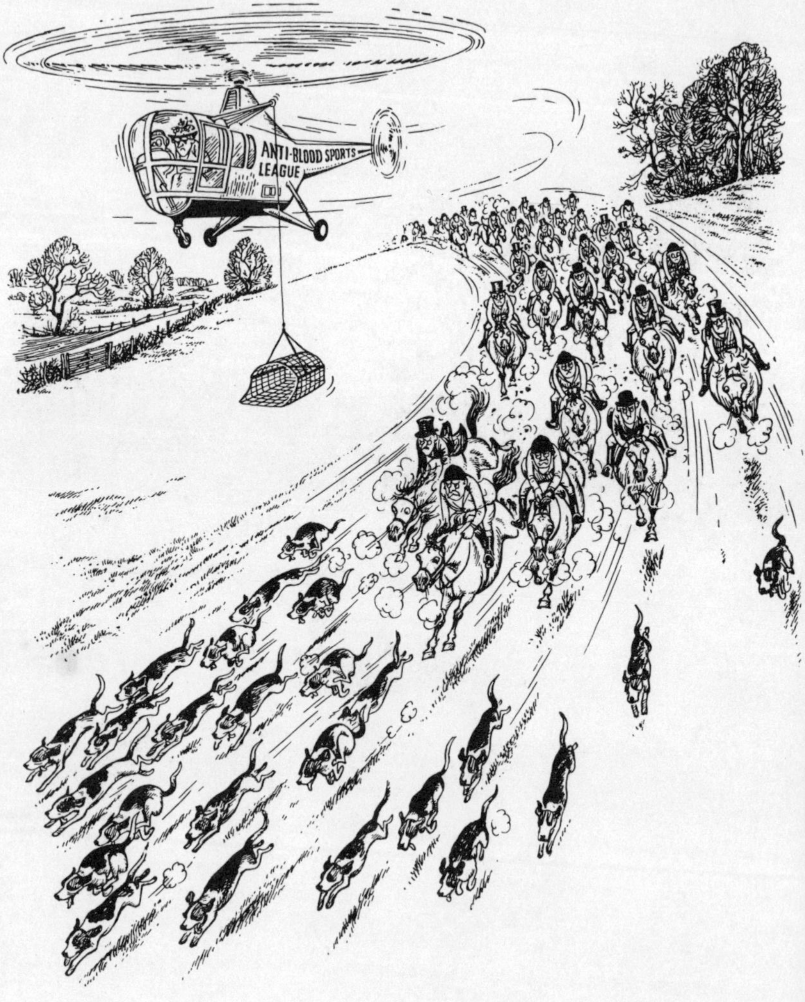
ANTI-BLOOD SPORTS
LEAGUE

"Charles! Did you ask anyone to meet you here this morning?"

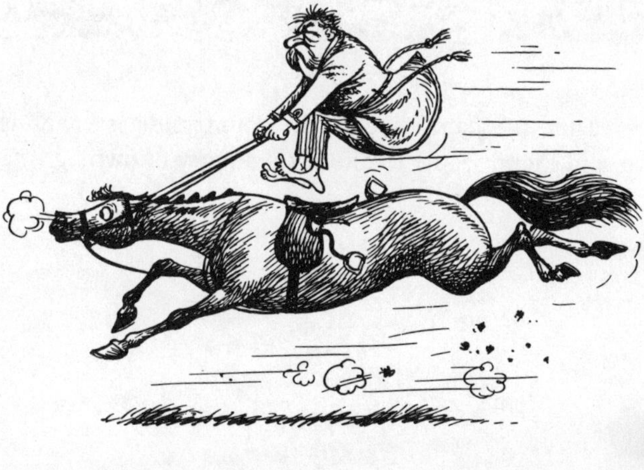

" Increasing mechanisation of the countryside is enabling more and more people to afford the luxury of owning . . . .

. . . a horse."

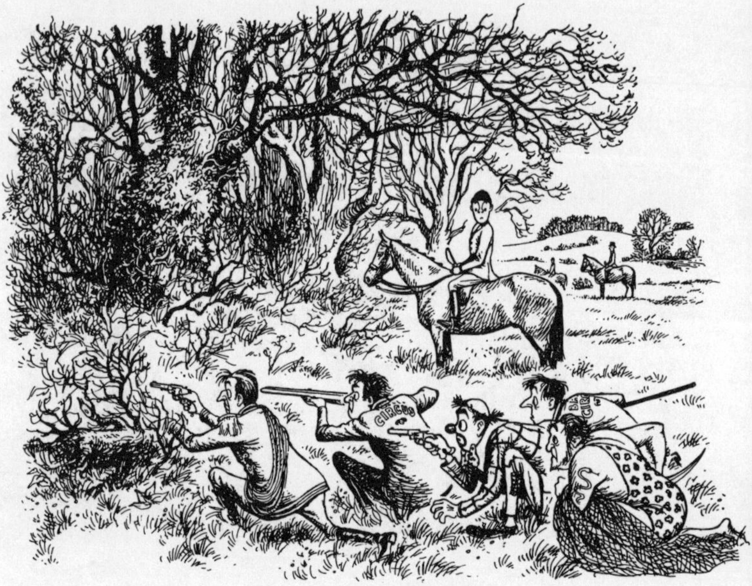

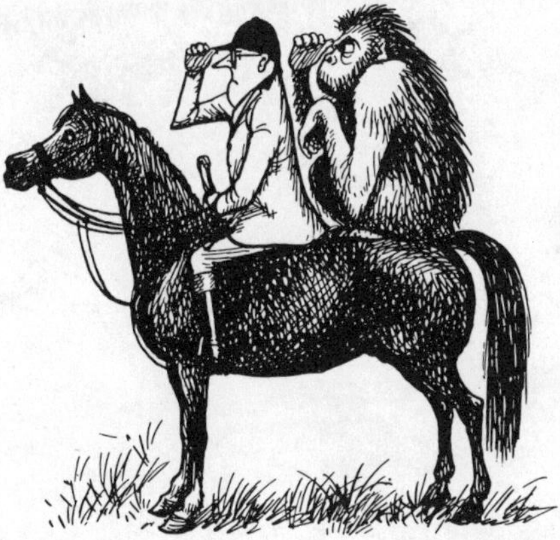

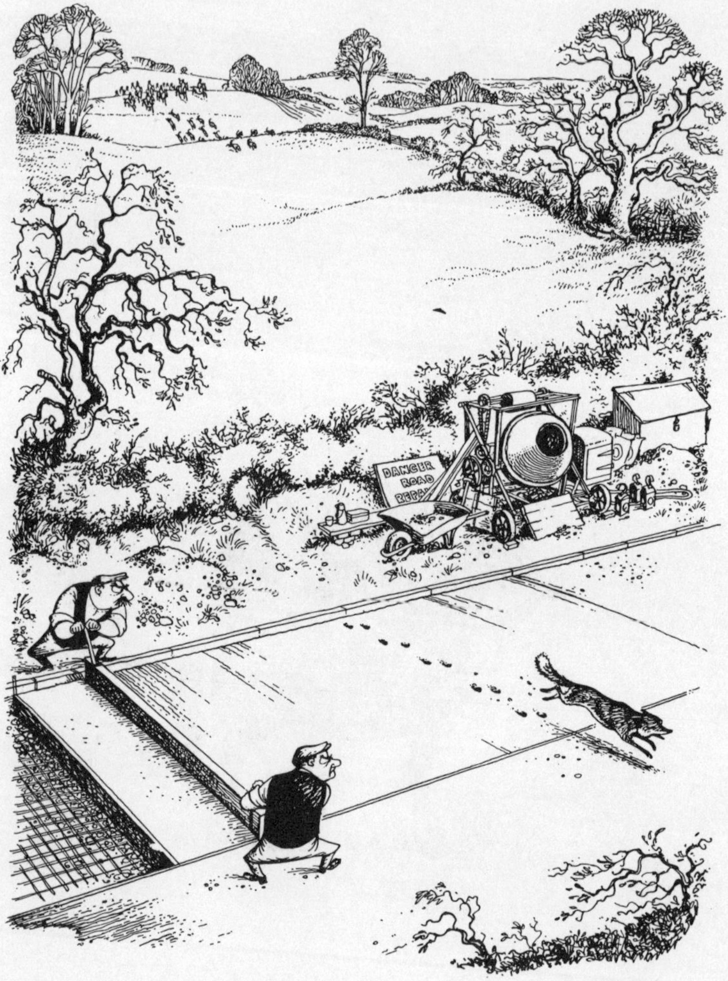
DANGER
ROAD

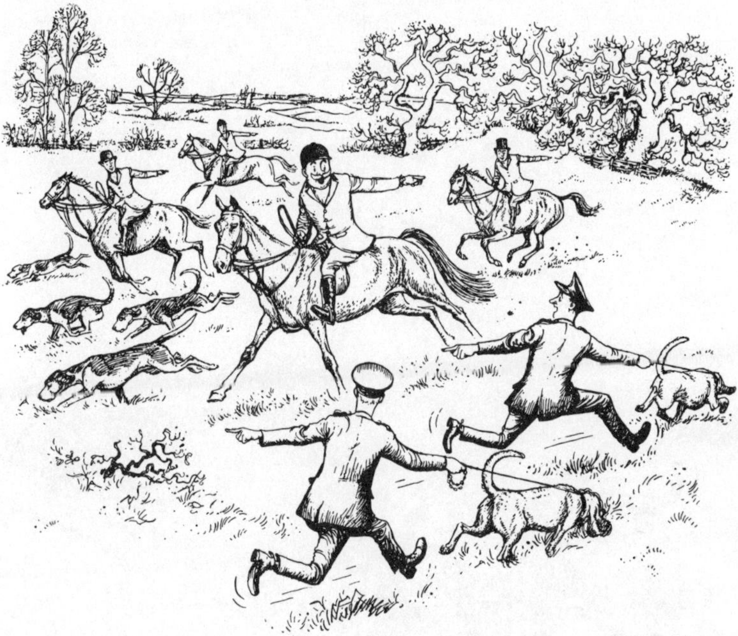

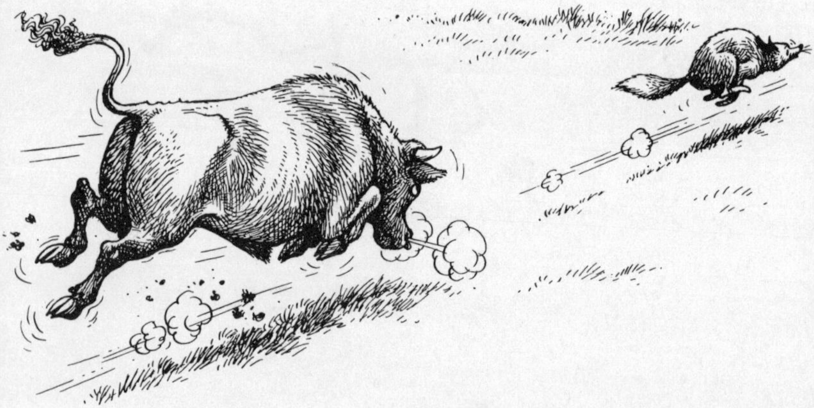

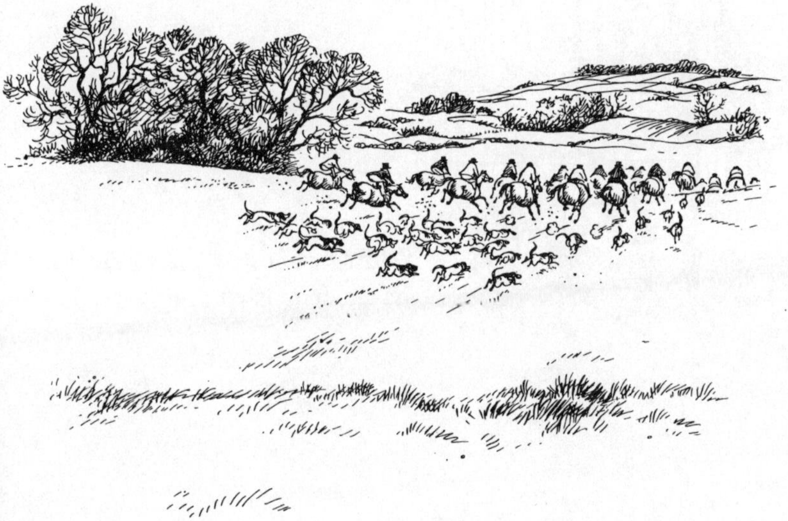

"Just *look* at it! 'Lacks initiative..
Easily dominated...'"

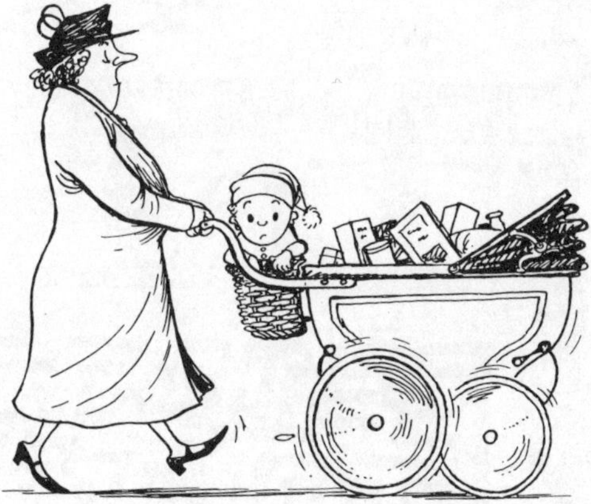

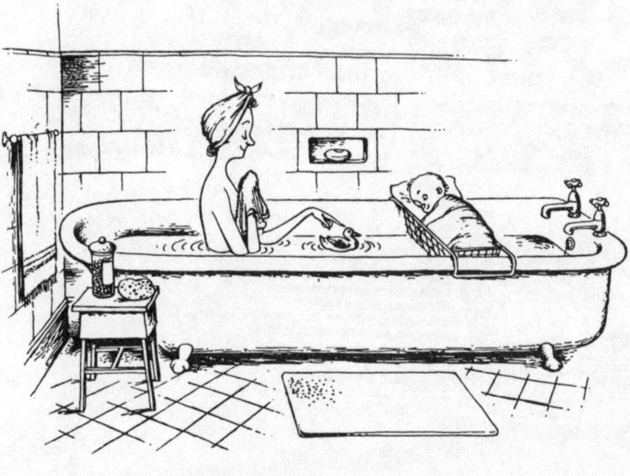

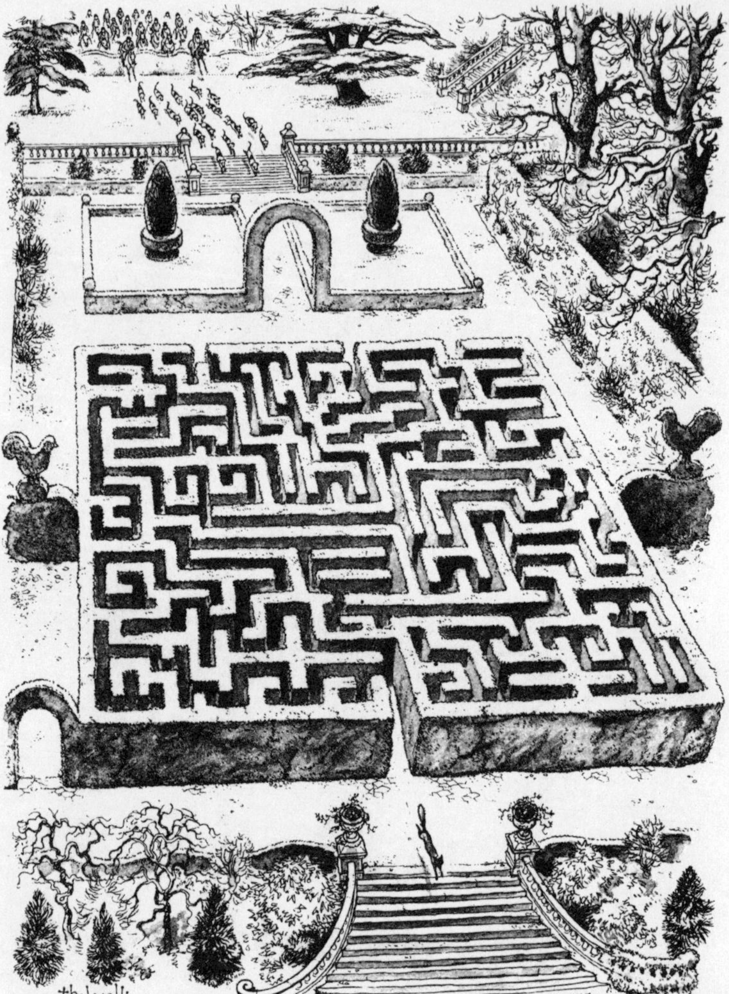
thelwell

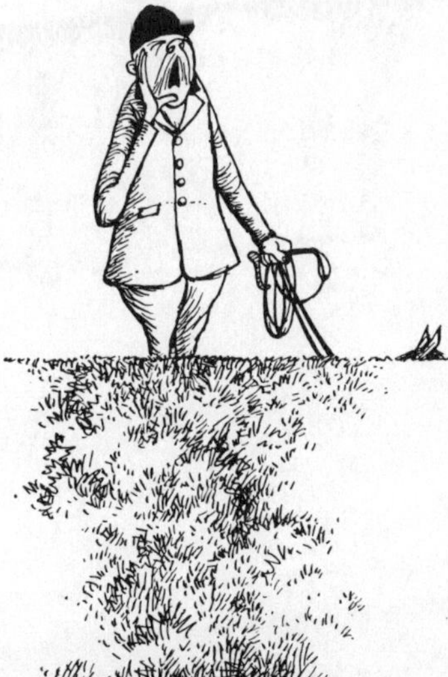

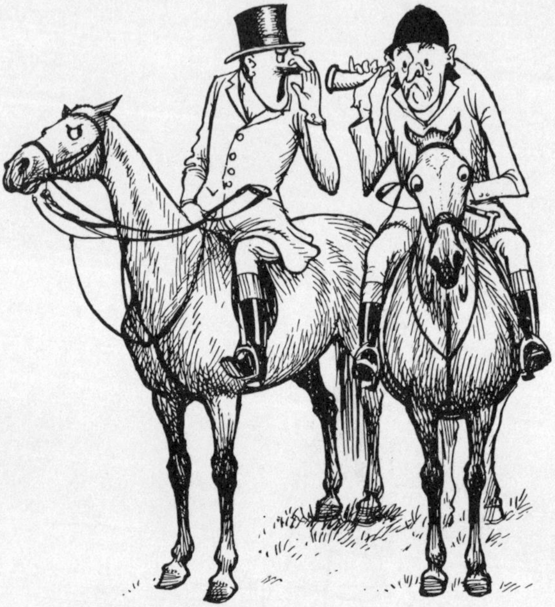

"Same again George."

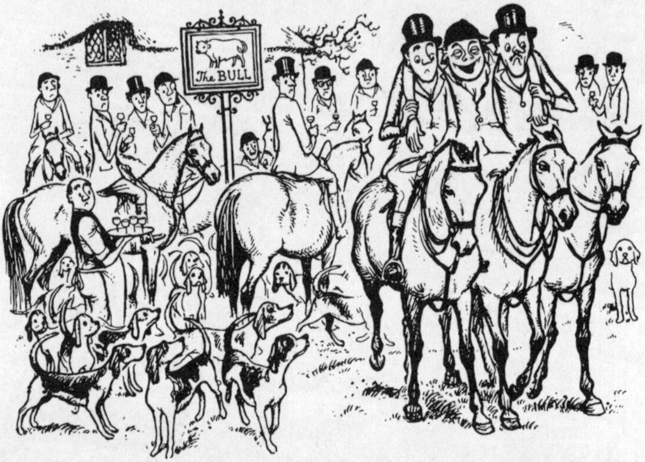
The BULL

Horses Mechanical

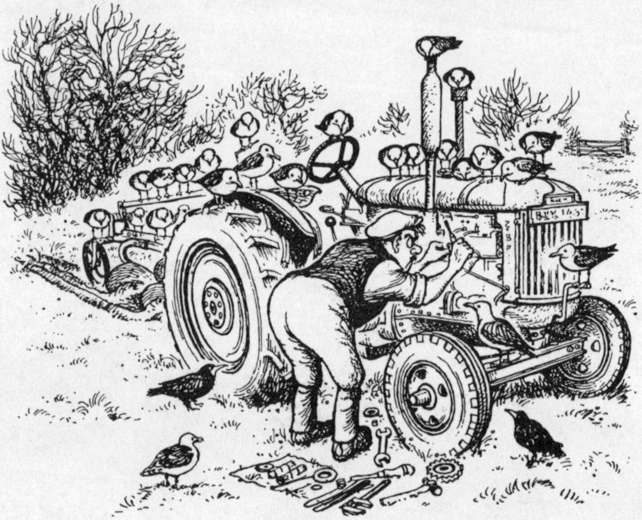

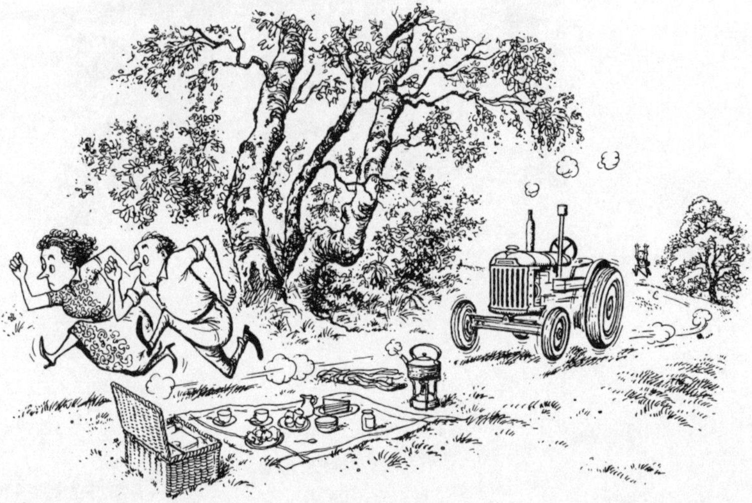

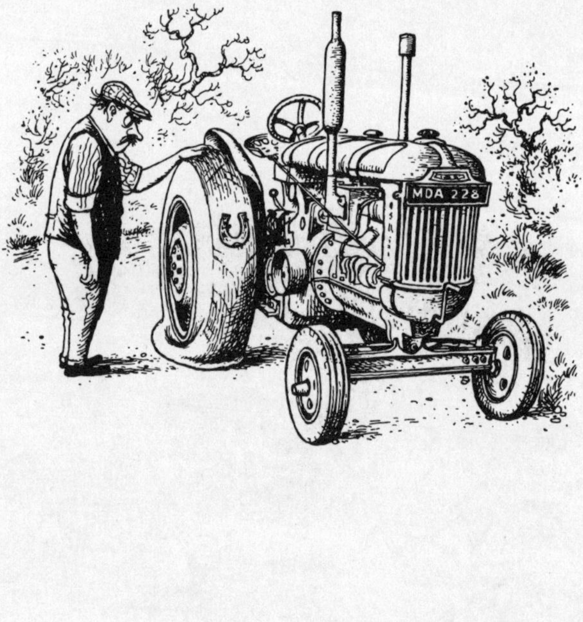
MDA 228

– And Otherwise

"Pretty-pretty."

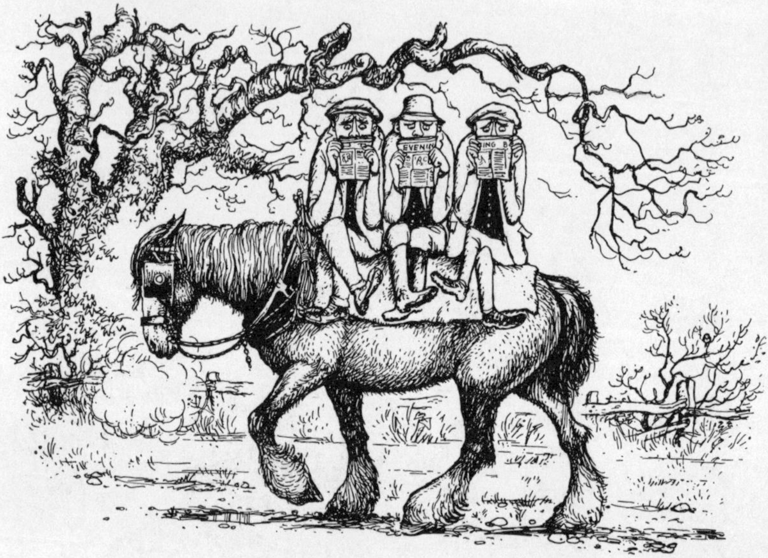

"Give Fred a shout as you go by—he's doing the traffic census."

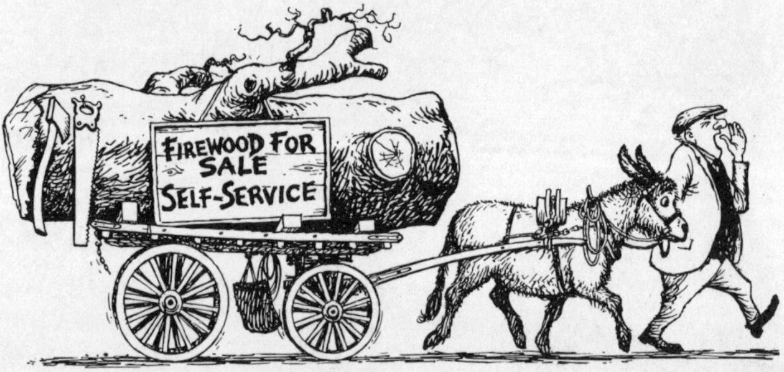
FIREWOOD FOR
SALE
SELF-SERVICE

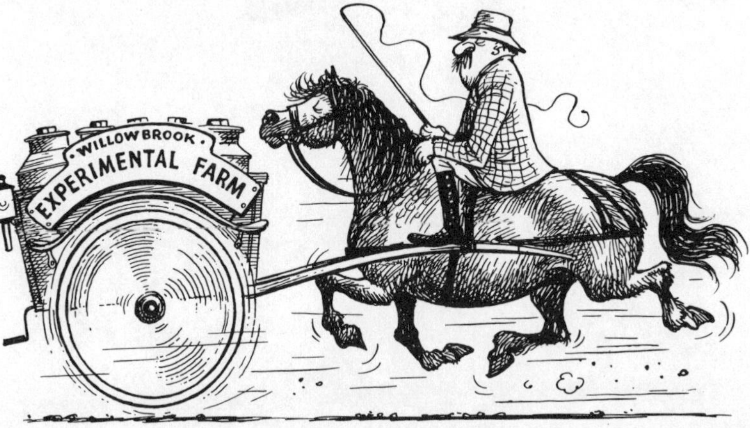
WILLOWBROOK
EXPERIMENTAL FARM

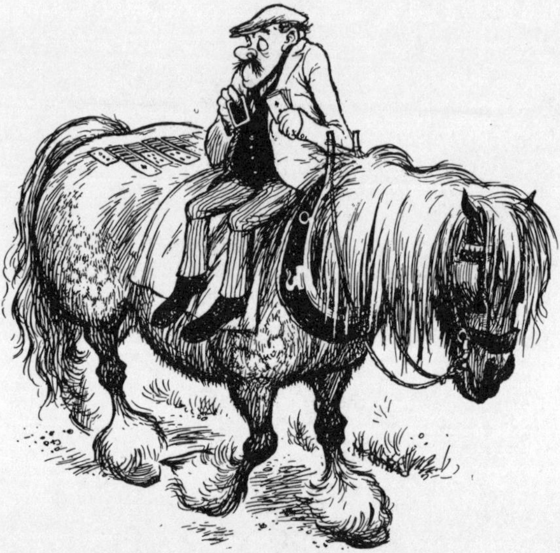

thelwell's
RIDING ACADEMY

To Cara,
For the next generation of Thelwell riders & ponies!
:) Joan

FOR
DAVID

thelwell's RIDING ACADEMY

New York, E. P. Dutton & Co., Inc., 1971

COPYRIGHT © 1963, 1964 BY NORMAN THELWELL
AND BEAVERBROOK NEWSPAPERS LTD
PRINTED IN GREAT BRITAIN

THIS BOOK IS BASED
ON A SERIES WHICH
APPEARED IN THE
SUNDAY EXPRESS

Contents

The Mount	page 7
First principles	21
The Academy	37
Care of your pony	53
Safety precautions	69
What to wear	85
Good manners	95
Academy pictures	111

"REMEMBER WHAT I TOLD YOU GIRLS, NEVER LET HIM SEE YOU'RE AFRAID."

THE MOUNT

"DO YOU HAVE ONE LIKE THIS IN DAPPLE GREY?"

SOME CHILDREN DISCOVER THE JOYS OF
RIDING AT A VERY EARLY AGE ......

... OTHERS PREFER TO WAIT UNTIL THEY ARE BIGGER.

ONCE IN THE SADDLE, HOWEVER, THEY
ARE ALL RELUCTANT TO LEAVE IT.

FINDING A RELIABLE PONY IS NOT EASY —

PROFESSIONAL ADVICE SHOULD BE SOUGHT...

FINDING A RELIABLE PROFESSIONAL
CAN ALSO HAVE ITS SNAGS.

YOU MUST BEAR IN MIND THAT FAT PONIES CAN BE HARD ON THE LEGS....

AND THIN ONES HARD ON THE JODHPURS

YOUNG ANIMALS CAN BE UNPREDICTABLE

AND OLD ONES JUST THE REVERSE

SOME INSTINCT WILL TELL YOU WHETHER YOU ARE GOING TO GET ON WELL TOGETHER

BUT **NEVER** BUY THE FIRST ONE YOU SEE.....

.... SOME DAY YOU MAY WANT TO SELL HIM.

IF YOU BUY A PONY THAT IS DIFFICULT TO CATCH —

        TAKE PLENTY OF LUMP SUGAR WITH YOU

AND EAT AS MUCH OF IT AS YOU CAN . . . . .

YOU WILL NEED ALL THE ENERGY YOU CAN GET.

YOU MAY LEARN A GREAT DEAL ABOUT A PONY BY LOOKING AT HIS TEETH

THIS OFTEN APPLIES ALSO.....

.... TO THE RIDER.

FIRST PRINCIPLES

"NO! NO! DEIRDRE, YOU'VE GOT THE WRONG FOOT IN THAT STIRRUP."

MOST CHILDREN MAKE VERY RAPID STRIDES AS SOON
AS THEY GET INTO THE SADDLE

ALTHOUGH STEADY PROGRESS IS LESS EASY TO MAINTAIN —

MUTUAL RESPECT MUST BE ESTABLISHED
              BETWEEN PONY AND RIDER

BUT IT SHOULD BE CLEARLY UNDERSTOOD WHO'S BOSS

NEVER SPEAK ANGRILY TO YOUR PONY

USE A KIND, GENTLE VOICE

IT WILL BE JUST AS EFFECTIVE

NEVER USE SPURS —

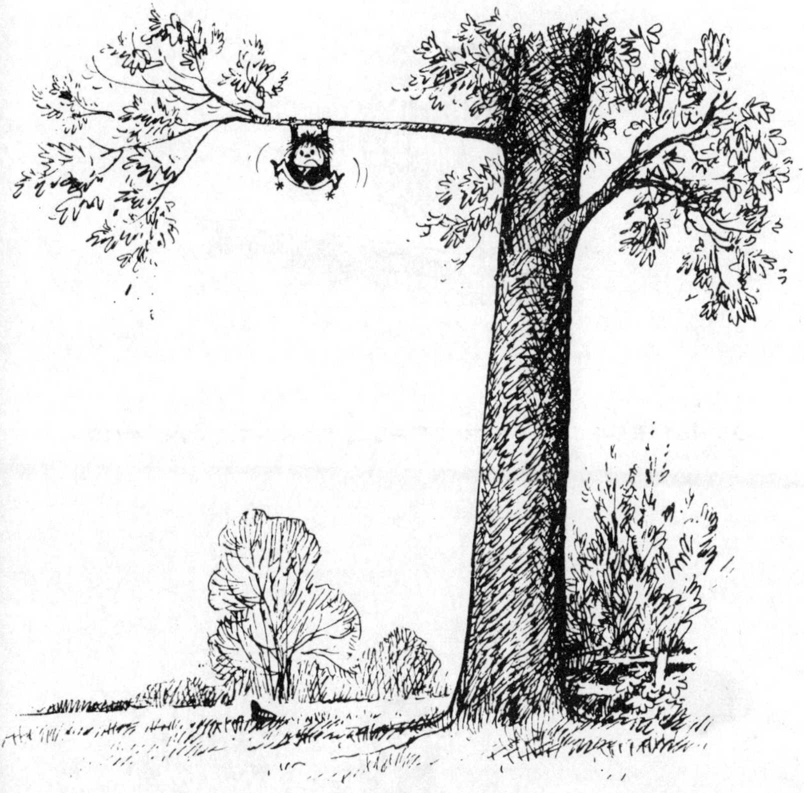

DO NOT EXPECT HIM TO BE ABLE TO READ YOUR MIND

SHOW HIM EXACTLY WHAT YOU WOULD LIKE HIM TO DO....

HE'LL BE VERY HAPPY TO OBLIGE YOU.

PONIES ARE WELL KNOWN FOR THEIR COURAGE

BUT THEY CAN BE SHY, SENSITIVE CREATURES ....

SO IF ANY OBSTACLE SHOULD CAUSE HIM TROUBLE...

...TAKE HIM BACK...

....REASSURE HIM....

35

... AND MAKE HIM DO IT AGAIN.

THE ACADEMY

"HAND UP THE ONE WHO SPOTTED MY DELIBERATE MISTAKE"

ALWAYS GET UP EARLY WHEN GOING TO RIDING SCHOOL —

YOU'LL NEED PLENTY OF TIME ....

.... TO WAKEN YOUR PONY

DON'T DAWDLE ON THE WAY ...

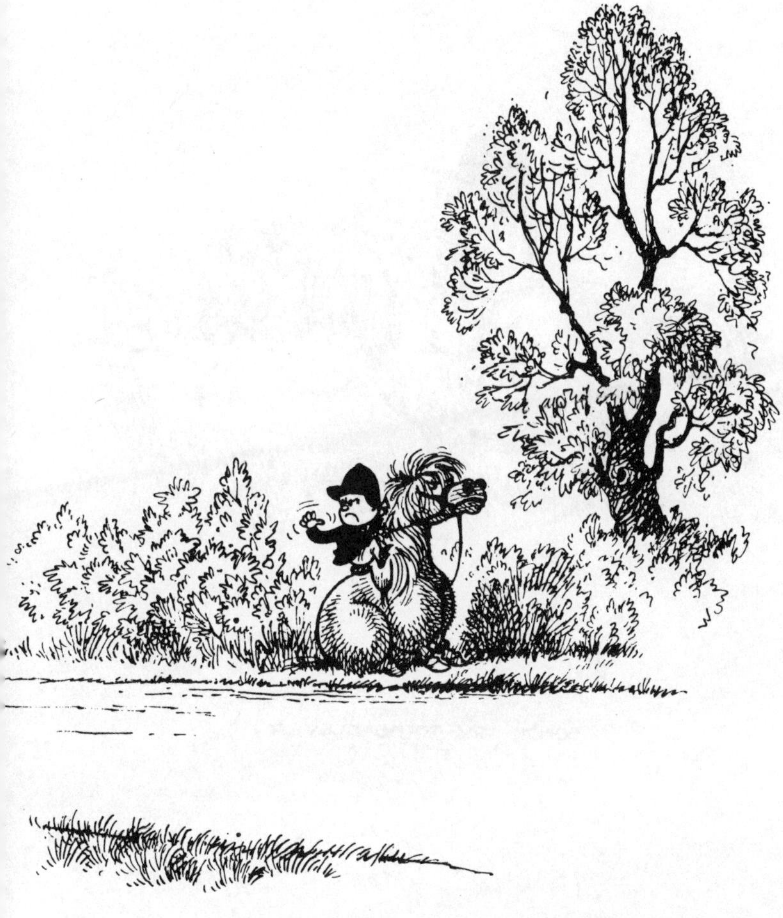

DON'T TRY TO BE CLEVER....

ALWAYS ENTER A RIDING SCHOOL BY THE FRONT GATE

MAKE FRIENDS WITH THE OTHER CHILDREN

YOU WILL LEARN A LOT FROM THEM

JUST SITTING ON A PONY'S BACK IS NOT RIDING —

SO WORK HARD AT YOUR STUDIES...

THERE WILL BE PLENTY OF TIME FOR PLAY

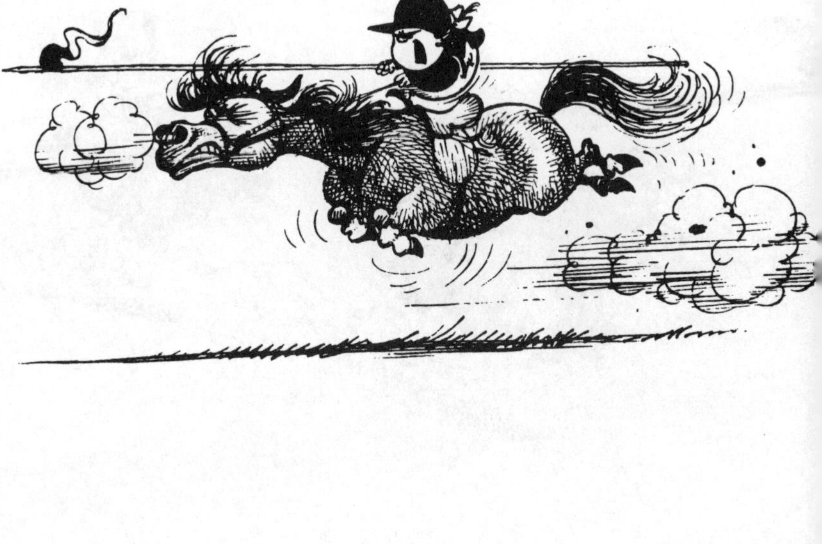

MOST INSTRUCTORS ENJOY A JOKE . . . .

BUT DON'T GO TOO FAR —

EXPULSIONS ARE DIFFICULT FOR ALL CONCERNED

CARE OF YOUR PONY

"DON'T JUST SIT THERE, DEAR - HURRY HOME BEFORE HE CATCHES A CHILL."

IT IS UNKIND TO RIDE YOUR PONY TOO FAST –

INSUFFICIENT EXERCISE, HOWEVER,
CAN LEAD TO EXCESSIVE FAT ..

SO GIVE HIM A GOOD LIVELY TROT EVERY DAY

THE RESULT WILL ASTONISH YOU.

NEGLECTING YOUR PONY'S COAT
IS A SERIOUS MATTER ...

... WHICH CANNOT FAIL ...

... TO CAUSE TROUBLE

IF FLIES BOTHER HIM IN HOT WEATHER . . . . .

TIE A SPRIG OF ELDER TO HIS BROW BAND . . .

HE WILL FIND IT A GREAT RELIEF

YOUR PONY'S SHOES SHOULD BE CHECKED REGULARLY

NEGLECT OF THIS SIMPLE PRECAUTION..

CAN LEAD TO SORE FEET.

YOU MUST LEARN TO RECOGNISE SIGNS
THAT YOUR PONY IS OFF COLOUR —

ROARING MAY INDICATE WIND TROUBLES...

... AND KICKING MAY MEAN A SORE SPOT .....

YOU WILL KNOW WHEN IT'S TIME
 TO CALL FOR THE VET

SAFETY PRECAUTIONS

"WHAT HAVE YOU DONE WITH HER THIS TIME?"

MAKE SURE YOU KNOW HOW TO PICK UP HIS FOOT...

LACK OF ABILITY IN THIS DIRECTION

MAY CAUSE YOU INCONVENIENCE

NEVER SHOUT 'GEE UP'

.... WHEN TEACHER IS MOUNTING

ALWAYS EXAMINE FENCES CAREFULLY
BEFORE JUMPING

THIS WILL ENABLE YOU TO BE READY...

FOR ANY EMERGENCY

NEVER TRY OUT NOVEL WAYS OF

GETTING INTO THE SADDLE

YOU'LL ENJOY QUITE ENOUGH VARIETY —

— GETTING OUT OF IT

IF ACCIDENTS ARE LIKELY TO OCCUR...

... AVOID WORRY ...

... BY MAKING SURE THAT THERE IS A QUALIFIED VET
IN ATTENDANCE

REMEMBER THAT THE RULES OF THE ROAD
                                    APPLY TO YOU...

AS WELL AS TO OTHER ROAD USERS

ALL ROAD SIGNS MUST
BE STRICTLY OBEYED

AND ALL HAND SIGNALS
CORRECTLY GIVEN.

SOME RIDERS LIKE TO HAVE A LOT OF
BANDAGES ON THEIR HORSES

THIS IS NOT ALWAYS AS POINTLESS....

... AS IT MAY APPEAR.

WHAT TO WEAR

"I'M BREAKING IN A NEW PAIR OF BOOTS"

A SMART TURNOUT IS
EXTREMELY IMPORTANT....

A RIDER'S ABILITY CAN USUALLY BE JUDGED

FROM HER APPEARANCE

THERE IS NO POINT IN BEING WELL
GROOMED YOURSELF, HOWEVER,

UNLESS YOU ARE PREPARED TO MAKE YOUR PONY...

... LOOK THE SAME

ROOMY JODHPURS ARE ADVISABLE...

AND A HARD HAT IS A MUST ..

ELABORATE WHIPS IMPRESS NOBODY —
   BUT REMEMBER ...

THE MOST ESSENTIAL ITEM

IN A RIDER'S WARDROBE

IS A GOOD PAIR OF BOOTS.

GOOD MANNERS

"DON'T BE SO MEAN, GEORGINA -
LET CHRISTABEL HAVE A TURN"

NEVER LET YOUR PONY NIP OTHER PEOPLES' . . . . .

IT IS BAD MANNERS FOR ONE THING....

AND CAN LEAD TO PAINFUL RESULTS

THE JUDGE'S DECISION MUST ALWAYS BE ACCEPTED AS FINAL

DO NOT BLAME YOUR INSTRUCTOR .....

... EVERYTIME SOMETHING GOES WRONG

DON'T PLAY WITH YOUR PONY IN THE GARDEN —

OR ALLOW HIM INTO THE HOUSE

DON'T MAKE FUN OF OTHER PEOPLE ....

... YOU MAY NOT BE PERFECT YOURSELF

YOU MUST NOT EXPECT YOUR MOTHER
TO KEEP YOUR PONY CLEAN

OR YOUR FATHER TO GIVE HIM EXERCISE

NEVER FORGET THAT WINNING PRIZES
                        IS NOT EVERYTHING . . . .

THOSE WHO MAKE THE ODD BLUNDER . . . .

ARE OFTEN MORE POPULAR.

ACADEMY PICTURES

" YOU HAVE TO APPROACH HER SLOWLY AND QUIETLY ....

"... HOLDING OUT A LOLLIPOP."

"IT'S JUST A QUESTION OF WHICH SHE BREAKS FIRST.
THE PONY OR HER NECK."

FILEY
TORQUAY
BLACKPOOL
SOUTHEND
BADMINTON
HORSE OF THE YEAR
WHITE CITY

" YOU'RE WASTING YOUR TIME DARLINGS —

        YOU CAN LEAD THEM TO THE WATER ...

... BUT YOU **CAN'T** MAKE THEM DRINK."

"PUTTING SHOES ON FOR YOU LOT IS PLAYING OLD HARRY WITH MY EYESIGHT"

"NEXT YEAR YOU CAN GO PONY TREKKING ON YOUR OWN"

"THEY KNOW PERFECTLY WELL THEY'RE SUPPOSED TO DRINK LEMONADE AS A STIRRUP CUP."

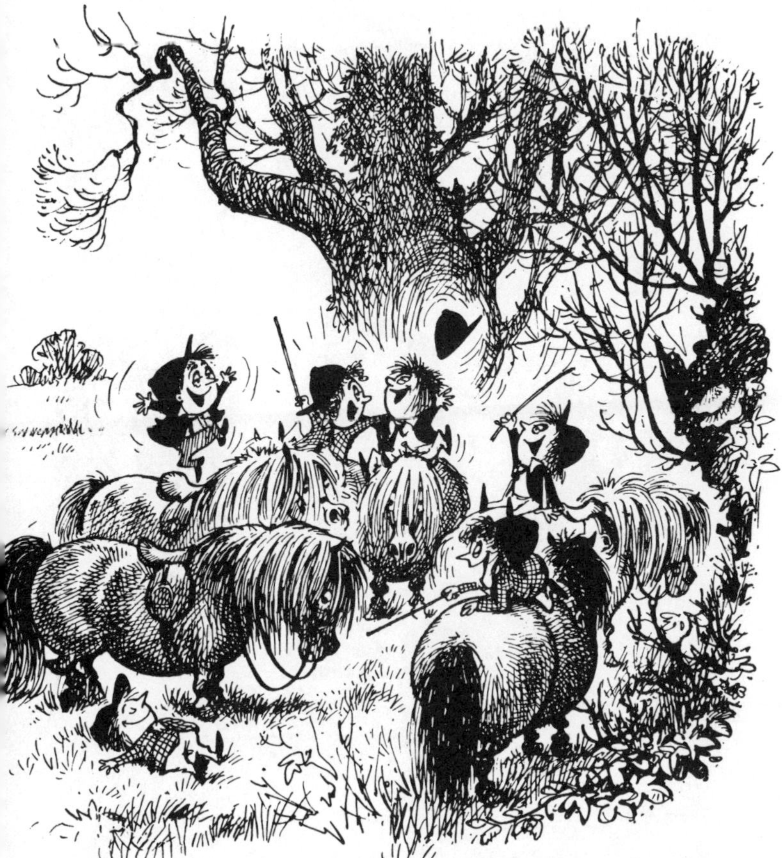

"THAT WAS MEAN – TELLING HER YOU'RE

ENGAGED TO DAVID BROOM."

"HE CAN MANAGE ON TINNED FOOD. WHY CAN'T YOU?"

"IF I LAY MY HANDS ON THOSE PERISHING KIDS"......"

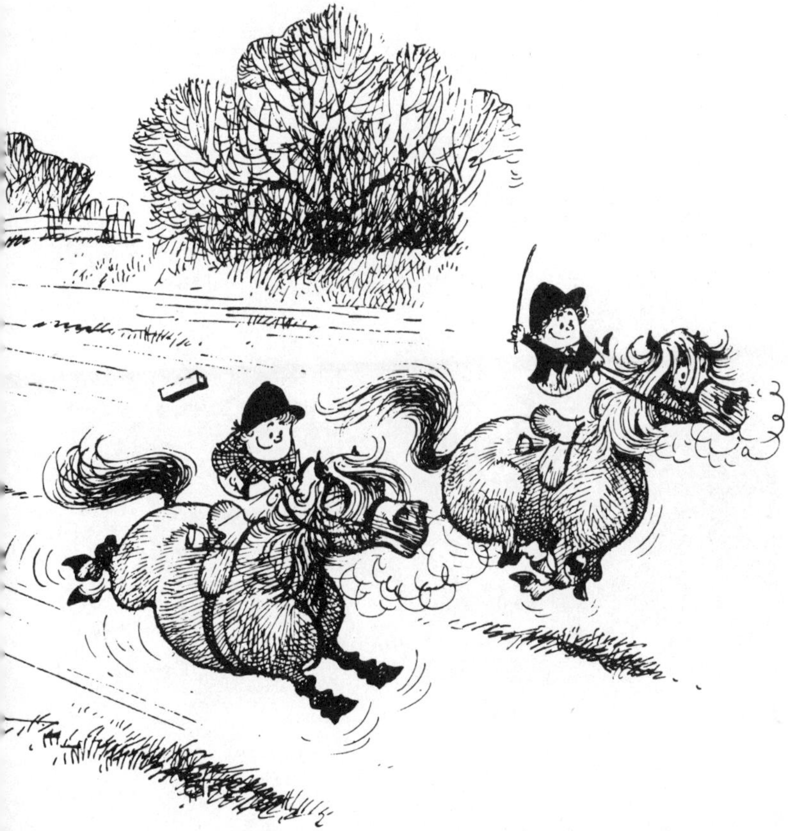

"HOW MANY TRADING STAMPS DID THEY GIVE YOU WITH HIM?"

"I WISH YOU WOULDN'T KEEP HIDING THEM IN YOUR BEDROOM. WE'LL HAVE THE WHOLE HOUSE OVERRUN WITH HOUNDS AGAIN."

"I'M SORRY MRS. CHADWICK
BUT WHEN YOUR DAUGHTER FELL
AT THE DOUBLE OXER,
I'M AFRAID SHE BROKE A LEG."